The Ultimate Blueprint of Mastering Money

Practical Strategies for Financial Success

By

Robertson Hood

Dedication

To my family and friends, who have always believed in me and supported my dreams.

Their love and motivation have been my guiding light throughout this journey.

This book is dedicated to you, for being my pillars of strength and unwavering source of inspiration.

Introduction

Welcome to a captivating journey—the pathway to financial mastery! With "The Ultimate Blueprint of Mastering Money: Practical Strategies for Financial Success," you hold in your hands the keys to unlock a world where financial abundance and prosperity become your new reality.

Imagine a life where money is no longer a source of worry or restraint, but a powerful tool that empowers and supports your dreams. Picture yourself making informed financial decisions with confidence, strategically growing your wealth, and creating a solid foundation for your future. This book is your roadmap to achieve just that.

In today's world, financial literacy has never been more crucial. Yet, many find themselves overwhelmed, uncertain, and trapped by their financial circumstances. Whether you're drowning in debt, struggling to save, or simply seeking to maximize your financial potential, this book is here to guide and transform your relationship with money.

"The Ultimate Blueprint of Mastering Money" goes beyond mere theory and provides you with actionable strategies to navigate the complexities of personal finance. Drawing upon years of experience, along with expert insights and research, this book offers practical wisdom that you can immediately apply in your life. From understanding your current financial situation to creating a comprehensive financial plan, from developing smart spending habits to building generational wealth, this book covers it all.

But beware, this isn't just another mundane financial guide. Within these pages lies a captivating narrative that engages, inspires, and motivates. It challenges conventional wisdom and delves into the psychological and emotional aspects of money, illuminating the profound impact our relationship with money has on our overall well-being.

Prepare to be captivated by stories of individuals who have risen above financial challenges and transformed their lives through these very strategies. Discover the secrets of highly successful individuals who have mastered the art of wealth creation and experienced true financial freedom. Their stories will ignite a fire within you, propelling you to break free from financial constraints and embark on your own journey toward financial dominance.

Are you ready to unlock the secrets of financial success? Are you eager to rewrite your financial story and reclaim your destiny? Your path to financial freedom begins now. It's time to embark on this transformative journey together and master the realm of money. Let's dive in and unlock the doors to your financial destiny!

CHAPTER ONE

Understanding Your Current Financial Situation

Understanding your current financial situation is very important for making informed decisions about your money and achieving your financial aims and goals. It entails assessing your income, expenditures, assets, debts, and overall financial health. Here's a encompassing guide to help you achieve a greater understanding of your financial situation:

Assessing Your Income

1. Frequency and Stability: Ascertain how frequent you receive income and its stability. Regular, steady income is preferable for financial planning.
2. Main Income Sources: Identify your primary or basic sources of income, such as salary/wage, business profits, rental income, or investments.
3. Summation of Income: Compute your total monthly and annual income by adding up all sources.

Evaluation Of Expenses

1. Flexible Expenses: Identify changeable expenses like entertainment, dining out, groceries/shopping, and discretionary spending.
2. Total Expenses: Adding up all your expenditures to understand your monthly and annual spending habits.
3. One-time Expenses: Consider any sudden or unexpected expenditures, such as medical bills, car repairs, or home maintenance.
4. Constant Expenses: Itemize crucial expenditures that remain stable each month, such as loan payments, rent/mortgage, utilities and insurance premiums.

Analyzing of the Assets

1. Non-Liquid Assets:This include assets like vehicles, real estate, jewellery, and other assets with an appreciating value or resale value.
2. Liquid Assets: Ascertain the value of valuables that can be rapidly transformed into cash, such as savings accounts, checking accounts, and investments like stocks and bonds.
3. Total Asset Value: Compute all the total worth of all your valuables combined.
4. Retirement Accounts: Assess the individual retirement accounts (I.R.A's).

Understanding Your Debts:

1. Types of Debts:Separate between secured debts(e.g., mortgage, bus loans) and relaxed debts(e.g., credit card debt, particular loans).
2. Interest Rates: Note the interest rates on each debt, as advanced rates can significantly impact your financial health.
3. Yearly Payments: Determine the minimal yearly payments needed for each debt.
4. Total Debt Owed: Adding up all your outstanding debts to understand your total debt burden.

Assessing Your Financial Health:

1. Net Worth: Compute your net worth by subtracting your total liabilities (debts) from the total assets(valuables). A positive net worth indicates financial stability.

2. Budget Surplus/Deficit: Compare your total income to the total expenditures. A surplus means you're spending less than you earn, while a deficit signals overspending.

3. Debt-to-Income Ratio: Divide the total monthly debt payments by your gross monthly income to assess your debt burden.

4. Emergency Fund: Evaluate the availability of your emergency savings to cover unforeseen expenditures and financial emergencies.

Setting Financial Goals

Setting financial goals is an important step towards achieving financial stability and success. This is how you can set effective financial goals:

1. Identify your priorities: Start by determining what matters most to you financially. Do you want to become debt-free, save for a down payment on a house, start a business, or retire comfortably? Clarifying your priorities will help you set specific goals that align with your values and aspirations.

2. Make your goals SMART: SMART stands for Specific, Measurable, Attainable, Relevant, and Time-bound. Ensure that each of your goals meets these criteria. For example, instead of saying "I want to save money," you can make it SMART by saying, "I will save $5,000 for a vacation in the next 12 months by setting aside $416 per month."

3. Break down your goals: Large goals can be overwhelming, so break them down into smaller, manageable milestones. This will make your goals less intimidating and provide a sense of progress along the way. For instance, if your goal is to pay off $10,000 in credit card debt, break it down into paying off $1,000 per month or $250 per week.

4. Set short-term and long-term goals: It's important to have a mix of short-term and long-term goals. Short-term goals can be achievable within a year or

less, such as building an emergency fund or paying off a small debt. Long-term goals may take several years or even decades, such as saving for retirement or education expenses. Having both types of goals will help you stay motivated and focused.

5. Prioritize your goals: Rank your goals based on their importance and urgency. It's not always feasible to focus on multiple goals simultaneously, so prioritize which goals to tackle first. Consider factors such as interest rates, deadlines, and financial impact. For example, it may be more beneficial to pay off high-interest debt before saving for a vacation.

6. Create a plan: Develop a detailed plan for each goal. Determine the actions you need to take, the resources required, and the timeline for achieving each milestone. Break down your plan into actionable steps, such as cutting back on expenses, increasing savings contributions, or seeking additional income streams. Regularly review and adjust your plan as needed.

7. Track your progress: Monitor your progress towards your goals regularly. This will help you stay accountable and make adjustments if necessary. Use tools like budgeting apps, spreadsheets, or financial software to track your income, expenses, and savings. Celebrate milestones along the way to keep your motivation high.

Remember, setting financial goals is not a one-time event. Review and reassess your goals as your circumstances change. Be flexible and willing to adapt your goals as needed to stay on track towards financial success.

Monitoring and Adjusting:

1. Regular Review: Schedule periodic reviews of your financial situation to track progress and make necessary adjustments.

2. Lifestyle Changes: Adapt your spending habits and financial strategies as your circumstances evolve, such as changes in income, expenses, or goals.

3. Seeking Professional Advice: Consider consulting with a financial advisor for personalized guidance and expertise, especially for complex financial matters or major life transitions.

By thoroughly understanding your current financial situation and actively managing your money, you can make informed decisions to improve your financial well-being and work towards achieving your goals.

How To Improve Financial Position:

Improving the financial position is like giving financial health a boost. It may take time and effort, but the rewards are well worth it.
The following are what to do improve the financial position to the optimal

1. Follow Up Your Expenses: Know Where Your Money Enters. Start by following up your spending like a jingoist. Get a handle on where your hard-earned cash is entering and identify areas where you can cut back. Look for any gratuitous spending and find ways to reduce charges without immolating your quality of life. Those diurnal lattes? Perhaps it's time to bring the coffee machine out from the reverse of the kitchen cupboard and fund the savings.

2. Design a Budget
Designing a budget is your ticket to financial success. It's like choreographing your money moves. Allocate your income to different categories, like bills, savings, and splurges. Stick to your budget and watch your financial position improve.

3. Reduce Debt
Say farewell to debt like a master. Focus on paying off your high- interest debts first while making minimum payments on the rest. Look into strategies

like debt connection or negotiating better interest rates. You 've got this!

4. Toil for Extra Income

It's time to unleash your inner hustler. Look for openings to boost your earnings, analogous as taking on a side gig, freelancing, or investing in your chops to advance in your career. The spare income can help you pay off debt hastily and save further for the future.

5. Make an Emergency Fund and Give It Some Love

Makeup that emergency fund like it's your financial BFF. Set down a portion of your income each month until you have got a buffer of three to six months worth of living charges. Having this buffer will give peace of mind and cover you from financial shocks.

6. Invest Wisely

Formerly you have erected a solid financial foundation, it's time to put your capitalist to work and watch it grow. But hold your horses , we 're not talking about throwing your hard- earned cash at every candescent investment that comes your way. We are talking about investing wisely. You can dip your toes into the stock request, dabble in bonds, or indeed take a vault into real estate. The key is to produce a diversified portfolio of investments that align with your trouble forbearance and financial pretensions. Do your disquisition, seek advice if demanded, and make informed opinions that suit your unique circumstances.

Evaluating your current financial position

1. Compute your net worth
Start by calculating your net worth, which is the difference between your means and arrears. Make a list of all your means, including your home, investments, savings accounts, and any precious effects. Also, list all your arrears, similar as outstanding loans, credit card debt, and mortgages. Abate your arrears from your means to determine your net worth. This will give you a shot of your current financial position and can serve as a birth for tracking your progress over time.

For illustration, if you have $ 200,000 in means and $ 150,000 in arrears, your net worth would be $ 50,000. Understanding your net worth can help you gauge your financial health and make informed opinions about saving for withdrawal.

2. Dissect your cash inflow
It's essential to have a clear understanding of your income and charges. Start by tracking your yearly income from all sources, similar as your payment, rental income, or any other sources of income. Also, list all your yearly charges, including fixed costs like rent or mortgage payments,

serviceability, insurance decorations, and variable charges like groceries, dining out, entertainment, and optional spending. By assaying your cash inflow, you can identify areas where you can cut back on charges and increase your savings.
For example, if you discover that you spend a significant portion of your income on dining out or entertainment, you can make a conscious effort to reduce these charges. Turning those finances towards your withdrawal savings can make a significant impact in the long run.

3. Review your debt situation. Assessing your debt is pivotal for financial planning. Make a list of all your outstanding debts, similar to credit card balances, pupil loans, and auto loans. Take note of the interest rates and yearly payments for each debt. Prioritize paying out high- interest debts first to save on interest payments and free up more finances for withdrawal savings.
For illustration, if you have a credit card balance with a 15 interest rate and a pupil loan with a 5 interest rate, concentrate on paying off the credit card debt first. Once that debt is cleared, you can allocate the finances towards your withdrawal savings or paying off the lower- interest pupil loan.

4. Estimate your withdrawal accounts
Assess your current withdrawal accounts, similar as 401(k) s, IRAs, or pension plans. Review your donation quantities, investment performance, and freights associated with each account. Consider

adding your donation rate, especially if your employer offers a matching contribution.

However, consolidate them to streamline your savings strategy and potentially reduce freights, If you have multiple withdrawal accounts. For case, if you have multiple old 401(k) accounts from former employers, consolidating them into a single IRA can simplify your withdrawal savings and give better investment options.

5. Consider working with a financial counsel or advisor

If you are doubtful about how to assess your financial situation or develop an effective withdrawal savings plan, consider working with a good financial counsel. A financial counsel can help you dissect your current situation, set realistic pretensions, and produce an acclimatized plan to boost your withdrawal savings.

Flash back, assessing your current financial situation is a pivotal step in the trip toward a secure withdrawal. By understanding where you stand financially, you can make informed opinions, identify areas for enhancement, and produce a solid plan to maximize your withdrawal savings.

Calculate Your Debt-to-Income Ratio

In addition to your credit score, your debt- to-income(DTI) rate is an important part of your overall financial health. Calculating your DTI may help you determine how comfortable you're with your current debt, and also decide whether applying for credit is the right choice for you. When you apply for credit, lenders estimate your DTI to help determine the threat associated with you taking on another payment.

Use the information below to calculate your own debt- to- income rate and understand what it means to lenders. How to calculate your debt- to- income ratio. Your debt- to- income ratio (DTI) compares how important you owe each month to how much you earn. Specifically, it's the chance of your gross yearly income(before levies) that goes towards payments for rent, mortgage, credit cards, or other debt.

To calculate your debt- to- income ratio.

Step 1

Your debt- to- income ratio is calculated by adding up all your yearly debt payments and dividing them by your gross yearly income. Add up your yearly bills which may include:

Yearly rent or house payment, Yearly alimony or child support payments Pupil, bus, and other yearly loan payments, Credit card yearly payments(use the minimal payment).

Other debts

Note: Charges like groceries, serviceability, gas and your levies generally are not included.

Step 2

Divide the total by your gross yearly income, which is your income before levies.

Step 3

The result is your DTI, which will be in the form of a chance. The lower the DTI, the less parlous you are to lenders.

Identifying financial strengths and weaknesses

SWOT analysis is a strategic planning tool used to identify the Strengths, Weaknesses, Opportunities and Threats affecting a business or an organization. An intriguing variation on SWOT analysis is the financial SWOT analysis, which provides sapience into those same four areas, but with a financial focus.

In this composition, we will look at the basics of financial SWOT analysis, including what it is, when to use it, and how to use it!

FINANCIAL SWOT ANALYSIS

Financial SWOT analysis is a business analysis tool that helps to identify the financial Strengths, Weaknesses, Opportunities, and Threats of an organization or business. It's an adaptation of SWOT analysis — which analyzes those same traits without a financial focus — generally used in fiscal or financial planning.

Looking at the four areas of SWOT analysis in depth:

STRENGTH: These are effects that play to a business ' benefit. In the case of financial SWOT analysis, this may include large cash reserves or positive yearly cash inflow.

WEAKNESSES:These are effects that play to a business ' detriment. For financial SWOT analysis, exemplifications include lots of debt or negative yearly cash inflow.

OPPORTUNITIES: These are effects which could profit the business, but don't presently. Financial exemplifications include possible cash investments or new profit aqueducts.

THREATS: These are effects which could disadvantage the business, but don't presently. Examples of financial SWOT analysis include non-paying guests or interest rate hikes.
Financial SWOT analysis is designed to give an overall picture of an organization or business current and implicit financial standings. It helps to understand how an association or organization is faring financially at present(thanks to the Strengths and Weaknesses linked), and offers insight into

implicit events that might dramatically change its finances(the Opportunities and Threats).

This can help an organization to plan both financially in agreement to transnational duty laws, by knowing what earnings and charges to anticipate, and strategically, in knowing how to pivot to optimize its financial standings.

When to Use Financial SWOT Analysis

Like other business analysis tools, financial SWOT analysis can be used at any stage before or during a business adventure. For illustration, companies might use financial SWOT analysis to estimate a new business occasion, with the idea of relating what the associated benefits and threats are from a financial perspective.
On the other hand, companies could use financial SWOT analysis to estimate their current financial standings and any prestigious opportunities and threats, so as to optimize their business plan for the future.

How to Use Financial SWOT Analysis

Conducting a financial SWOT analysis is more or less like conducting any other SWOT analysis. This means the bulk of the work lies in relating applicable Strengths, Weaknesses, opportunities and Threats.

Relating Strengths, Weaknesses, Opportunities and Threats

It's generally easiest to start with the Strengths and Weaknesses, since these represent the current standings of the business. For a financial SWOT analysis, Strengths and Weaknesses can frequently be set up by looking at balance wastes, which show earnings and charges. This will allow you to determine whether the business has a positive or negative cash inflow, which can be a major Strength or Weakness. Other financial Strengths and Weaknesses to look at include means, arrears, and the readiness for borrowing money.
In particular, it's useful to identify whether the business can easily apply for loan or borrowing money, and at what interest rates.

Making Together The Mystifications

Once you have linked the factors that could affect the business, it's time to collect, and latterly interpret the SWOT analysis. In collecting a SWOT analysis, review the Strengths, Weaknesses, Opportunities, and Threats linked and ensure they are sufficiently significant. It's insolvable to cover everything in a single analysis, so aim to concentrate on the most important issues. After laying out and reviewing factors from these four areas, decide whether a report is necessary.

However, it may be worth collecting all the findings into a single document, If the SWOT analysis is to be participated with others.

However, whatever notes made will be sufficient, If not. Eventually, begin interpreting the SWOT analysis in order to develop practicable strategies.

For illustration, look at the Strengths linked and determine whether fresh work is necessary to maintain them. Also, consider how any Weakness might be resolved or worked around. Also, look at how Opportunities can be grasped and Threats avoided. While SWOT analysis is useful in its own right — as a frame to identify current standings and implicit unborn scripts — its true value is in enabling you to find these practicable perceptivity. As a result, conduct a SWOT analysis, but be sure to leave acceptable time to pick out these perceptivity and produce practicable strategies. Knowing clearly is half the battle, but acting on that knowledge is the pivotal alternate half.

Setting financial goals based on your aspirations and lifestyle

Setting financial goals that align with your aspirations and lifestyle is crucial for creating a fulfilling and sustainable financial plan. Here are some steps to help you set goals based on your unique circumstances:

1. Reflect on your aspirations: Take some time to envision your ideal future and consider what financial milestones you need to achieve to make that vision a reality. Think about the lifestyle you want to lead, the experiences you want to have, and the impact you want to make. This will help you identify the financial goals that are meaningful to you.

2. Consider your current lifestyle: Assess your current financial situation and lifestyle. Evaluate your income, expenses, and spending habits. Look for areas where you can make improvements or adjustments to support your aspirations. This will help you understand how your current choices are affecting your financial journey and identify areas where you can prioritize your goals.

3. Set specific and realistic goals: Make sure your goals are specific, measurable, and attainable within a reasonable timeframe. Consider both short-term and long-term goals. Short-term goals might include things like paying off a certain amount of debt or saving for a vacation, while long-term goals could involve saving for retirement or buying a home. Based on your aspirations and current circumstances, set goals that you believe are realistic and achievable.

4. Align goals with your values: Your financial goals should reflect your values and what you prioritize in life. For example, if you value experiences and

travel, your goals might involve saving for specific trips or creating a travel fund. If you are passionate about making a positive impact, you may set goals to donate to a cause you care about or start a social enterprise. Aligning your goals with your values will give you a sense of purpose and motivation.

5. Evaluate trade-offs: When setting financial goals, you may need to make trade-offs and prioritize certain goals over others. Consider the potential costs and benefits of each goal and determine how they fit into your overall financial plan. Assess whether achieving certain goals now may postpone or hinder other goals. This will help you make informed decisions and balance your aspirations with practicality.

6. Break down goals into actionable steps: Once you have identified your goals, break them down into smaller, actionable steps. This will make them more manageable and provide a clear roadmap for achieving them. For example, if your goal is to save for a down payment on a house, your actionable steps could involve creating a budget, cutting expenses, and increasing savings contributions.

7. Track progress and make adjustments: Regularly review and track your progress towards your goals. This will aid you stay accountable and make amendments if needed. If you encounter challenges or changes in your circumstances, be

flexible and willing to adapt your goals accordingly. Revisit and adjust your goals as necessary to ensure they remain realistic and relevant to your aspirations and lifestyle.

Remember, financial goals should be personal and customized to your unique aspirations, values, and circumstances. By setting goals that align with your lifestyle, you'll be more motivated and have a clear direction towards financial success.

CHAPTER TWO

The importance of financial plan

Financial planning is a methodical approach that helps you manage your money and expenses and plan for saving and investing.
Financial planning allows you to achieve your financial pretensions, be it buying a family home, saving for children's education, having a comfortable withdrawal or going on a dream vocation be it locally or internationally. It also prepares you for unlooked-for situations and extremities like falling sick, losing your job, or having to patch your house.

In short, financial planning is a methodical approach that helps you manage your money and expenses and plan for saving and investing. A financial plan covers budgeting, insurance, mortgages, investments, levies, and withdrawal and estate planning. It also prepares for implicit threats or risks and unlooked-for events.

How Financial Plan Look Like

Financial planning reflects upon your pretensions, fiscal situation, risk forbearance and prospects, also calculates how important cash you'll need at different intervals and draws a strategy to achieve your financial goals. Financial plans are as unique as each existent. They must feed everyone's requirements and solicitations. Your plan should tell your own story and connect the blotches of your life.

Benefits of Financial Planning

Financial planning gives you peace of mind, which does wonders for your health and emotional well-being.
1. It helps you identify and prioritize your financial aims and goals.
2. It identifies the financial stressors in your life, as well as possible risks or threats and extremities and proposes solutions.
3. It recognizes your spending habits and introduces results to increase your cash inflow.

How To Create a Financial Plan

A good financial plan addresses several crucial factors.

1. Set Financial pretensions

What should your life look like in 5, 10 and 20 years?

Are kiddies in the picture?

Do you want to enjoy a house?

How do you imagine withdrawal?

2. Track Your Cash Flow

An accurate picture of your money allows you to direct it to short-, mid-, and long- term goals.

3. Prepare for unforeseen circumstances (Emergency)

A foundation of any financial plan is putting cash down for exigency charges.

4. Pay Your Debt

Launch by repaying your most precious debt and plan to pay the rest over time. Barring the debt burden gives you more disposable income.

5. Assess and Manage Pitfalls or Risks

Risks come in numerous shapes and sizes. Some pitfalls can be addressed through insurance, others through savings and investments.

6. Invest

Your investment strategy is the foundation of your financial plan. A good investment strategy draws on your pretensions and cash inflow protuberance and balances the risks you are willing to take with the return you need. We should be involved in all aspects of financial planning but we do not know everything. A trusted financial diary can support you with every step to produce a plan acclimatized to your conditions and requirements.

What Do Financial Planners Do

Financial planners help you meet your short- and long- term goals. They assess your financial situation, understand what you want, and help you plan to get there. They identify a strategy to help you reduce spending, pay debt, and save and invest for the future. They relieve you from managing your investment, conforming your investment strategy to the changing profitable and market outlooks.

Assessing short-term and long-term financial goals What does financial goals mean? Financial goals are targets or effects a person wants to achieve with their money or finance in the future. These goals differ from person to person and may change over the course of a person's continuance.

Financial goals can be for different lengths of time, and for different quantities of money. Having a budget, or a financial plan, goes a long way in helping someone achieve their financial goals. Savings and spending habits, earning income and investing are all effects to consider when trying to reach a financial goal.

Financial goals examples

Financial Goals can change over the course of a continuance. For example, a grown-up may be saving to put a down payment on a house or planning for withdrawal.
Some examples of financial goals for students could be establishing credit or starting an emergency fund.

Setting Financial Goals

Setting financial goals is important to make sure money is being spent and saved wisely. A person needs to think about what they hope to negotiate and plan accordingly.

Financial goals fall into three introductory orders:
1. Short term financial goals
2. Mid term financial goals
3. Long term financial goals

Short Term Financial Goals

Short term financial goals are effects someone is hoping to achieve in the coming three months. Going on holiday or buying a new appliance are short term goals. Saving money in a bank account is generally the stylish option to finance short term goals.

Short Term Goals Example

Some examples of short term financial goals include:

1. Starting an emergency fund

This is maybe one of the most important financial goals and should be started as beforehand as possible. Having money in a savings regard for injury, illness or other unanticipated extremities is essential.

2. Paying off debt

Debt, similar to credit card debt, can be precious. Spending redundant money each month on interest payments means lower money that can be put toward more important effects like saving and investing toward your goals.

Mid Term Financial Goals

Mid-term financial goals refer to specific objectives or targets that individuals or households aim to achieve within a timeframe of roughly three to five years. These goals typically involve saving, investing, or allocating funds toward significant expenses or milestones that are expected to occur within that time frame. They serve as stepping stones towards long-term financial stability and often require consistent planning, saving, and potentially investing to accomplish.

Mid-term financial goals typically span between three to five years and can include objectives like:

1. Saving for a down payment on a house or car.
2. Building an emergency fund equal to three to six months of living expenses.
3. Paying off significant debt like student loans or credit card balances.
4. Investing in education or professional development to enhance career prospects.
5. Saving for a major vacation or sabbatical.
6. Contributing to retirement accounts to secure future financial stability.
7. Starting or growing a business venture.
8. Saving for a child's education fund or future expenses.

Long Term Financial Goals

Long-term financial goals are objectives or targets that individuals or households aim to achieve over an extended period, typically spanning beyond five years and often throughout their lifetime. These goals involve planning and saving for significant financial milestones or aspirations that may require substantial time and effort to accomplish.

Long-term financial goals include retirement planning, purchasing a home, funding a child's education, building substantial wealth, or achieving financial independence. Achieving long-term financial goals often involves strategic planning, consistent saving and investing, and adjusting strategies over time to adapt to changing circumstances.

Examples of long-term financial goals:
1. Retirement Planning: Saving and investing to ensure a comfortable retirement with sufficient funds to maintain desired lifestyle.
2. Homeownership: Saving for a down payment, paying off a mortgage, and eventually owning a home outright.
3. Children's Education: Funding higher education expenses for children or grandchildren, including tuition, books, and other related costs.
4. Financial Independence: Building enough wealth to have the freedom to pursue passions and interests without being reliant on employment income.

5. Estate Planning: Ensuring assets are managed and distributed according to personal wishes, including providing for heirs or charitable causes.
6. Travel and Adventure: Saving for extensive travel experiences, such as world tours or extended vacations during retirement.
7. Starting a Business: Building capital and resources to launch and sustain a business venture, whether it's a small startup or a larger enterprise.
8. Healthcare Expenses: Saving for potential future medical costs, including long-term care or unexpected medical emergencies.

9. Philanthropy: Establishing funds or foundations to support charitable causes and make a positive impact on society.
10. Legacy Building: Leaving behind a financial legacy for future generations, such as establishing trusts or endowments.

Difference between long term and short term financial goal

Short- term financial goals are those that you hope to achieve within the coming time or so, while long- term financial goals are those that you hope to achieve further down the line generally five times or further.   It is important to have both types of goals, as they serve different purposes.
Short- term goals tend to be more palpable and specific, while long- term goals may be more general and aspirational.
Short- term goals can help you stay motivated and concentrated on your overall financial plan. They can also act as stepping stones to your long- term pretensions. For example, if you are saving for a house deposit, your short- term thing might be to make up a savings pot of 5,000 within the coming time.
Long- term goals, on the other hand, can keep you motivated by giving you a commodity to aim for in the future. They can also help you concentrate on the bigger picture and make better financial decisions.

For example, if you want to retire at 55, your long-term goal might be to have a pension pot of 500,000.

The stylish way to achieve your financial goals is to produce a plan and stick to it. This means setting aside money each month to reach your targets. Automatizing your savings can help to make this process more easier and aid you stay on track. Still, there are plenty of free online coffers and tools that can help, If you are not sure where to start. The key is to get started and review your progress regularly to make sure you are on track.

Most people have financial goals. But not everyone understands the difference between short- term and long- term financial goals.
Short- term financial goals are those that you hope to achieve in the coming time or so. For example, you may want to save up for a down payment on a house or a new auto.   Long- term financial goals are those that you hope to achieve in five years or more. For example, you may want to save for withdrawal.   The time frame for achieving your goals isn't the only difference between short- term and long- term financial goals. Short- term goals are generally less precious than long- term goals. That is because you have less time to save for a short- term thing.
Long- term goals are generally more precious than short- term goals. That is because you have enough time to save for long- term goals.

You also need to consider the risks associated with each type of thing. Short- term goals are generally less risky than long- term goals.
That is because you have less time to make miscalculations with short- term goals.
Long- term goals are generally more risky than short- term goals.
That is because you have enough time to make miscalculations with long- term goals.

Typical example, let's say you want to retire at age 65. You have 30 years to save for retirement. However, you have a much longer time horizon than someone who starts saving when they are 45 years old, If you start saving when you are 35 years old.
This means that the 45-year-old has a shorter time horizon to make up for any miscalculations they make with their savings. They also have a shorter time horizon to take advantage of emulsion interest.
The 35-year-old, on the other hand, has a longer time horizon. This means they have further time to make up for any miscalculations they make with their savings. They also have enough time to take advantage of emulsion interests. The nethermost line is that short- term financial goals are generally less risky than long- term financial goals. But that does not mean that short- term goals are always less expensive than long- term goals.

It's important to understand the difference between short- term and long- term goals so that you can make stylish decisions for your situation.

Financial planning setting short term and long term financial goals

When it comes to financial planning, it is important to set both short- term and long- term financial goals.

This will help you stay on track with your finances and ensure that you are always working towards a specific financial goal. Short- term financial goals are generally effects like saving up for a down payment on a house or auto, or paying off high- interest debt. These are goals that you can generally achieve within a year or two.

Long- term financial goals are more like withdrawal savings or saving for your child's education. These are goals that will take several years to achieve.

The first step in setting financial goals is to figure out what your priorities are.
What do you want to achieve in the short term?
What do you want to achieve in the long term?
Once you know your priorities, you can start setting specific goals.
Example, let's say your priority is to save for a down payment on a house. Your short- term thing could be to save $10,000 within the coming two

years. Your long- term goals could be to have a down payment saved up within five years.   Once you have your goals set, the coming step is to produce a plan of action. How are you going to save the money you need to reach your goals?
Are you going to cut back on charges?
Are you going to start investing?
Creating a plan of action will help you stay on track with your goals and make progress towards achieving them.
One final tip for setting financial goals is to review them regularly. This will help you see how far you've come and whether or not you need to make any changes to your plan. Reviewing your goals also allows you to acclimate them as your requirements change. Still, talk to a financial expert, If you are not sure where to start with setting financial goals. They can help you figure out what your priorities are and produce a plan to help you reach your goals.

Analyzing Short-Term vs. Long-Term Financial Impact on your Business Decisions

In the fast- paced world of the Green Industry, making informed financial opinions is vital for long- term success. Still, it's important to consider the impact on both the short term and the long term when assessing these opinions. In this book, we will explore nine pivotal reasons why it's essential for businesses to fully assess the goods on both the short term and the long term before making significant financial opinions.

1. Financial Stability and Sustainability
Analyzing the short- term and long- term financial impact helps ensure the stability and sustainability of your business. For illustration, let's say you're considering taking on a large design that requires significant open costs. By analyzing the short-term cash flux impact and assessing the implicit long-term profit and profitability, you can assess whether the design aligns with your financial goals and ensures the long-term sustainability of your business.

2. Profitability Optimization
By assessing short- term and long- term impacts, you can identify openings to optimize profitability. For example, suppose you're meaning raising your service rates to increase immediate profit. However, through careful analysis, you may discover that a farther strategic approach, analogous as investing in technology to improve effectiveness, can lead to advanced long- term profitability by attracting further guests and reducing costs.

3. Resource Allocation
Analyzing the short- term and long- term impact helps you allocate resources effectively. For

example, if you're considering expanding your team to handle increased demand, assessing the short- term cost of hiring and training new workers against the long- term benefits of increased productivity and service capacity can help you make informed resource allocation opinions.

4. Risks Mitigation

Assessing the short- term and long- term financial impact helps identify and palliate implicit risks. For example, if you're considering entering a new market segment that presents immediate growth openings but also carries implicit long- term risks, such as increased competition, analyzing the short- term earnings against the long- term sustainability of the business can help you make a balanced decision.

5. Cash Flow Management

Understanding the short- term and long- term goods of financial opinions aids in effective cash flux operation. For example, suppose you're assessing the purchase of a new outfit that requires a significant open investment. Analyzing the short- term impact on cash flux and the implicit long- term benefits, such such as increased effectiveness and reduced conservation costs, allows you to manage cash flow effectively while icing long- term profitability.

6. Return on Investment(ROI) Assessment

Analyzing the short- term and long- term impact allows you to assess the ROI of different opinions directly. For example, if you're considering investing in marketing campaigns, assessing the short- term costs against the implicit long- term benefits, such as increased brand awareness and customer accession, helps you determine the ROI of the marketing investment and make an informed decision.

7. Strategic Planning

Considering the short- term and long- term implications of financial opinions is critical for strategic planning. For example, if you're assessing the accession of a contender to expand your request reach, analyzing the short- term integration challenges against the long- term request dominance and increased customer base helps you align the decision with your strategic pretensions and vision for the future.

8. Competitive Advantage

Analyzing the short- term and long- term impact of opinions enables you to gain a competitive advantage in the Green Industry. For example, if you're meaning to administer technology systems for design operation and client communication, analyzing the short- term performance costs against the long- term benefits of better effectiveness, customer satisfaction, and competitive positioning helps you make a decision that enhances your competitive edge in the market.

9. Stakeholder Confidence
Fully analyzing the short- term and long- term financial impact demonstrates sound financial operation to stakeholders such as investors, lenders, and mates. For example, if you're considering additional funding for expansion, conducting a comprehensive analysis of the short- term and long- term financial projections, ROI potential and risk factors helps inculcate confidence in stakeholders and enhances your credibility as a financially responsible business.
In the dynamic terrain of businesses, analyzing the short- term and long- term financial impact is vital for making informed opinions that drive sustainable growth and success. Keep these points in mind the coming time you are faced with making a move.

Prioritizing goals and setting a timeline

How to Prioritize Your Work

Still, work prioritization allows you to determine the important tasks that need to be dived first and can help you stay flexible as new assignments cross your path, If you have a lot on your plate. Do not worry about having enough time to complete everything that needs to get done in record time. This section will help you understand colorful prioritization styles and how to shift gears for critical matters that affect your workflow.

Make a Task List

Build a list of all the tasks you need to complete, writing them out and keeping them in one place. Your list will serve as a visual memorial of your goals. When creating your list, ideally, you will organize tasks into several orders. Your daily list should include your short- term goals and the high-goal tasks that need to be completed on a tighter deadline, similar as by the end of the day. A daily or yearly list of goals will keep you on track for mean systems, while your long- term list keeps your big picture goals in mind.

Determine Task Deadlines

With your task list in hand, you next need to determine your deadlines. In some cases, that will be easy to figure out, as an external force — like your master or a customer — will bear a due date. For other particulars on your to-do list, identify every step needed to accomplish them and estimate the likely required time it will take you to get them done.
Can you complete a task within a workday or do you need more time?
It's important to review these particulars with a critical lens so that you can set an accurate timeline

for each task. Also, assign yourself a deadline for each item and work on those with the nearest deadline.
Those should be your highest priority.

Assess the significance of Tasks
As you review your to-do list and assign deadlines, assess the significance of each task. To do this directly, you will need to have a deeper understanding of your professional goals and company culture.
Also, check in with your heads, workers, co-workers, and customers or clients for feedback on tasks and to determine your most important work. Understanding the perspective of all stakeholders involved will help you make stylish choices when prioritizing your goals.

Complete Tasks and Reevaluate Your Task List
As you complete tasks, reevaluate your task list. Life is changeable, especially when it comes to business. You never know what new tasks will pop up as you are working on a task. Be set to acclimatize your deadlines to problems and new priorities that arise. Inflexibility will take you far as you set goals and work to achieve them.

Strategies for budgeting and saving

Budget strategy

A budget strategy is a formal approach to managing a collection of finances. Multitudinous people use budget strategies in their particular lives to ensure their expenses don't exceed their income. Others use budgeting strategies to help reach financial goals, like buying a new car or saving a certain amount for retirement. Most professionals also use budgeting strategies at work to help ensure a department or association can pay for all its expenses and potentially invest in future opportunities.

Some effective budget strategies you can use to achieve your goals

You can try several budgeting strategies to find one that suits your goals and conditions.

1. Deduction budgeting

Deduction budgeting is one of the simplest forms of budgeting. To use this system, you add all your monthly expenditures and subtract that total from your overall monthly earnings. The amount you have left over is what you can use for savings and entertainment.

2. Cash budgeting

Cash budgeting, which some people call envelope budgeting, has you use actual cash for purchases and expenditures rather than managing digital currency. Having cash constantly helps those who have trouble imagining their money in digital form track it more easily.

With a cash budgeting system, rather than putting your paycheck into your bank account, you cash it and use the physical bills and coins to pay for your charges. Some people put the specific amount of cash they need for expenses, like rent and utility, into sealed envelopes until they pay those bills, so they can avoid spending it on other things.

3. Commensurate budgeting

With a commensurate budgeting strategy, you divide all your expenditures into three orders, which are savings, conditions and wants. From there, you determine which chance of your income you want to devote to each of these orders.

Also, you can divide your income into those orders accordingly.

4. Two- bank budgeting

Using the two-bank budgeting strategy, you pay yourself before paying any other expenses. This allows you to add to any savings plans or buy any particulars you want. One effective system of this strategy is to open a checking account in which you deposit your paycheck.

Also, set up an automatic transfer from that account to a secondary bank account, leaving a small portion of your paycheck behind in the original account. You also can live off the money in your secondary account and leave the savings from your original account for unforeseen circumstances or other purchasing goals.

5. Automatic budgeting

Automatic budgeting allows you to benefit from the erected- in budgeting systems most banks give. Consider setting up automatic bill pay and automatic transfers. This ensures you pay all your expenses on time and meet your savings goals without having to make any factual payments or deposits.

6. Online or app budgeting

Most operations help you track your spending and effectively produce a substantiated budget that meets your goals and conditions. Budget operations are software operations that sync to your financial accounts and total all your information in one place, so you always know the amount of money you are spending and earning. Consider using one of these programs to help you establish a unique budgeting system specifically for you and your spending patterns.

7. 50/30/20 budgeting

The 50/30/20 system is a traditional budgeting strategy that uses rates to help you manage your money. Principally, with this strategy, 50% of your income goes to your conditions or non-negotiable rudiments, like rent and utility, 30% goes to your wants or particular expenses, like dinner out and other entertainment, and 20% goes toward savings and paying off any debt you have. People who want to buy a property or produce an emergency savings account can benefit from using the 50/30/20 budgeting strategy.

8. Multi-account budgeting
The multi-accounting budgeting system is a digital interpretation of the cash envelope budgeting strategy. Using this system, you open multiple bank accounts and devote each to a specific expenditure or savings goals. You can use automatic transfers to shoot the applicable quantum of money to each account and automatic bill pay programs to insure you pay your expenses on time.

9. Zero-grounded budgeting
A zero- grounded budgeting approach is another traditional strategy that focuses on ensuring you have enough of your income set away to cover your necessary expenses. With this system, you deduct expenditures from your yearly income until you have a remainder that completely funds whatever is most important that month. This means you are working toward a zero- waste situation with your finances, ensuring you regard for all of your income.

10. Savings and emergency budgeting
Still, a savings and emergency budgeting strategy may be largely effective, If you want to maximize

your savings. With this system, a certain chance of your income goes into a general savings account you can use for specific purchasing goals, like a house or a car.

Another chance goes into an emergency fund for unanticipated expenses, like a car repair or loss of a job.

11. Repaid disbenefit card budgeting A strategic budgeting approach for those who dislike carrying cash but struggle to limit their credit card use is the repaid disbenefit card budgeting strategy. It functions as a combination of the cash envelope system and the multi-account budgeting strategy, but it uses reimbursed disbenefit cards for daily expenses rather than using cash or a card for your bank account. This ensures you can not overdo your account and spend outside of your means.

12. Priority budget

A priority budget includes determining your priorities rather than counting on destined priorities others set. You make a list of all your charges and spending priorities and arrange them in the order that is most important to you. From there, you can determine how important money you want to devote to each order.

Tips for maintaining your budget

Deciding on a budget strategy is an excellent first step in effectively saving your money. Do ensure you follow the guidelines you establish in your budget and can help you meet your short-term and long-term budgeting goals. Then there are many tips to help you maintain your budget.

1. Track spending
One of the stylish ways to maximize your budget is to track your spending and see where you can make changes to meet your short-term and long-term financial goals.
2. Review and update.
Regularly review the budget you've created to ensure you are spending within the limits. Update and change your budget as demanded to reflect spending patterns and changing pretensions.
3. Establish goals.
Ensure the goals you set for your budget are realistic and attainable.
Consider using the SMART goals to help you produce effective financial goals.
4. Use tools.
Use tools like apps and online plutocrat trackers to help you get a clear sense of your spending and saving.

5. Stay motivated.
Regularly remind yourself why you are using a budget by looking at your long-term goals to help you stay motivated to save.
6. Reduce credit card use.

It can be easy to overspend with a credit card. However, consider using cash or disbenefit (Prepaid) cards rather to keep you from spending further money than you have, If you frequently spend more than what you have.

Some Ways to Save Money

Use these simple money-saving tips to induce ideas about the swish ways to save money in your day-to- day life.

1. Count Your Debt
Still, start with your debt, If you are trying to save money through budgeting but still carrying a large debt burden. Not convinced? Add up how important you spend servicing your debt each month, and you will snappily see. Once you are free from paying interest on your debt, that money can easily be put into savings. A particular line of credit is just one option for consolidating debt so you can pay it off.

2. Set Savings goals
One of the ways to save money is by imaging what you are saving for. However, set saving targets along with a timeline to make it easier to save, If you need provocation. Want to buy a house for three years with a 20% down payment?
Now you have a target and know what you will need to save each month to achieve your thing.

3. Pay Yourself First

Set up a machine transfer from your checking account to your savings account each payday. Whether it's $50 every two weeks or $500, do not cheat yourself out of a healthy long- term savings plan.

4. Stop Smoking
No, it is not easy to quit, but if you smoke a pack and a half every day, that could amount to thousands of bones a time that you can realize in savings if you quit.
According to the Centers for Disease Control and Prevention, the chance of American grown-ups who smoke cigarettes is now below 12% — join the club!

5. Take a Staycation
Though the term may be trendy, the allowed behind it's solid rather than dropping several thousand on airline tickets overseas, look in your own vicinity for fun recesses close to home. However, look for cheap flights in your region, If you can not drive the distance.

6. Spend to Save
Let's face it, avail costs rarely go down over time, so take charge now and weatherize your home. Call your utility company and ask for an energy audit or find an experienced contractor who can give you a whole- home energy effectiveness

review. This will range from easy advancements like sealing windows and doors all the way to installing new insulation, siding or Energy Star high-impact appliances and products and indeed solar panels. You could save thousands in utility costs over time.

7. Utility Savings

Lowering the thermostat on your water heater by 10°F can save you between 3% and 5% in energy costs. And installing an on-demand or tankless water heater can deliver up to 34% savings compared with a standard storage tank water heater.

8. Pack Your Lunch

An obvious money- saving tip is changing everyday savings. However, bringing lunch from home costs only $3, also over the course of a time, If buying lunch at work costs $10. Do try to opt for home made foods instead of buying at work.

9. Open an Interest Bearing Account

For the ultimate of us, keeping your savings separate from your checking account helps reduce the tendency to borrow from savings from time to time. However, consider products with advanced yield rates like a CD or money market account for indeed better savings, If your goals are more long-term.

10. Annualize Your Spending

Do you pay $20 a week for snacks at the dealing machine at your office?

That is $1,000 you are removing from your budget for soda pop pop and snacks each time. Suddenly, that habit adds up to a substantial sum. As you apply these tips into your financial life, flash reverse that where you save your money is important too. Regularly move the money you save out of your checking account into your savings account, where you will be less likely to touch it before you reach your goals.

Allocating resources effectively to achieve desired goals

Resource allocation is the process of strategically concluding and assigning available resources to a task or design in support of business objects.
In the terrain of account, allocation deals with the assignment of people and with their skills to specific tasks, also known as engagements. The substance of optimal resource allocation for any accountancy establishment is matching the right people, with the right experience, qualifications, and skills with the right client and task, at the right time.

Resource allocation vs Resource scheduling
Allocation also considers the availability, capacity, and utilisation of resources across an establishment but should not be confused with scheduling.

Scheduling is a vital part of the resource planning process and generally follows allocation. After relating and allocating resources predicated on the swish match of skills and experience for an engagement, a resource manager will subsequently record these resources for a specific time and task. The resource scheduling process should ensure that it schedules resources with the necessary skills, experience, and qualifications for the right task and at the applicable stage of the engagement.

Importance of Resources Allocation

Effective allocation should ensure work is divided inversely among all resources to help staff collapse Empower teams by ensuring resources have the skills, knowledge, and training necessary to complete allocated work ensure engagement performance is optimised by matching the right resources, to the right task, at the right time In the delivery of any design, poor allocation of resources will have a knock- on impact on overall performance.

Lacking the right skills or knowledge on a design can result in the loss of effectiveness, time, confidence, and provocation along the way. In account, an optimal allocation process is pivotal in order to empower teams, help collapse, and ensure engagement performance.

In this context, allocation is not only a crucial operation process, it's also a critical switch for growth and success. Constantly allocating the right resources to the right tasks at the right time is vital for successful and profitable client engagements. When an establishment allocates its resources, it matches the devoted resources to achieve client and business objects.

Benefits of Effective Resource Allocation

Getting it right is not always easy, but when done right, effective resource allocation can give multitudinous benefits. Some of the pivotal benefits include:

1. Staff retention

Poor allocation can contribute to a burned- out pool. A survey of 1,222 UK accountants and ACA scholars from the accountancy good charity CABA set up that two in five accountants feel too emotionally drained to work. When asked about the cause of the stress 33 reported either their work, career, or studies as the root cause. Using the right allocation process, an establishment can drive better utilisation, hand satisfaction, and retention simultaneously. An effective system will optimise resource utilisation rates without overfilling your people. Effective allocation styles help other suitable and available resources from being overlooked, icing tasks are assigned both fairly and strategically. In addition, by taking into account individual preferences, interests, and career aspirations when allocating work, your establishment can more support professional development and retention.

2. Client Satisfaction

Resource managers concentrate on assembling optimal teams, blending industry experience with the right skills and commissions for quality and effectiveness.

Stylish is a private generality, but clients will anticipate to see individualities with the right qualifications and experience assigned to deliver their engagements. That means those with applicable skills, insight, and knowledge applicable to the client's specific business and industry. This could include a combination of technical skills or sector experience, with particular ' soft skills ' demanded on top. But these skills do not each have to live in one person, position or time zone.

An optimal resource allocation system considers these details and identifies a team with the most suitable skills for each design stage. A resource management system that can use your people in the swish way, will benefit staff and client satisfaction likewise.

3. Profitable engagements

Allocating the right resource combinations for complex engagements demands thorough, up-to-date knowledge of your resources ' skills, capacity, and industry. It also requires the capability to directly predict the impact that resourcing opinions will have on engagement performance. In the long term, an effective allocation strategy can help your establishment to strike the right balance between over and under utilisation of resources. Maintaining this balance reduces the risks of overfilling your team or overspending on resources that are not demanded. Allocating the right resources to the right engagement.

CHAPTER THREE

Developing Smart Spending Habits

Identifying and curbing unnecessary expenses

Gratuitous charges are those that do not contribute to your essential conditions, goals or values and that can be reduced or barred without affecting your quality of life.

Effective Tips for Reducing Your Expenses

Follow these ways to identify gratuitous purchases and help lower your expenses. It's possible to have confidence in your budget, indeed in uncertain times. These ways can help you get a better handle on your money and save for a brighter future.

1. Know where your money goes.
Writing down what you spend for a week has been set up to improve financial confidence. So as to become more financially flexible, you should track your expenses. That's where budgeting comes in. Every budget begins with two vital numbers: your yearly expenditures and your yearly income. Produce a budget that tracks both your income and spending. This gives you a clearer idea of how your money is coming in and going out, and will allow

you to estimate your financial habits over time to see what kinds of patterns develop.

2. Make Spending categories

With your budget in place, make a list of your conditions, wants, and particular values of the goods that count most to you. Defining your values can help you budget for what's truly important, whether that's starting a business, giving back to the community, or spending time with your family. Essential particulars like rent or mortgage payments, groceries, and mileage will presumably take precedence over " fun " purchases, depending on your budget. Look at how much you 're spending on wants — gratuitous particulars that do not inescapably reflect your priorities and consider what you can live without for now.

3. Only spend on what matters most

Indeed though "fun" expenses may take a backseat, they can still be good for your internal health, so you should still include them in your budget. You can still save for and spend money on goods that are aligned with your particular values, like buying breakouts to surprise family or saving money for a class you want to take. By following a budget rested on your values, you will feel happier and further satisfied with your purchasing opinions, and it won't feel like a chore to save commercials to achieve goals.

4. Make the ultimate of " monthlies "

Recreating yearly costs can add up, so also are some tips to lower those charges. Consider temporarily suspending your spa class in favor of at- home exercises, breaking public transportation accounts, or concluding for groceries over takeout or delivery services, which can be more precious. Make a list and decide if there's anything you are willing to put on hold.

5. Eliminate impulse buys

Half of Americans say that they buy goods they do not really need. If your social scrolling generally turns into " Thanks for shopping, " find ways to cut down on unplanned expenses. Spontaneous purchases can unhinge your commercial goals. Be alive of what triggers this most for you, like those 50% off emails from your favorite attire store. Set an dispatch sludge so you do not see them unless laboriously shopping. When an appetite does strike, return to your list of values if that purchase does not align with your goals.

6. Save on interest where you can

Still, you know interest is a big part of your yearly payment, If you have a mortgage payment or car loan. However, see if refinancing could help you lower your interest payments over time, If money is tight. Alternately, if your income has not changed, consider making a fresh top payment or two while other charges are on hold. This helps you make equity, reduces the life of the loan, and minimizes interest paid.

7. Consider promptness

Some financial institutions have introduced forbearance options like promptness of machine loans during this time. However, check with your bank to see what options they can give you, If you need to. While you'll have to pay later, this can help you lower expenses for the present moment. You should avoid promptness if you are suitable, still, because you will still accrue interest during the promptness period, which eventually results in you paying further commercial interest.

Identifying and curbing unnecessary expenses

Simple Ways to Cut Unnecessary Spending

Tips to Cut Back on Your Charges and Make the Most Out of Your Budget.

One of the more delicate aspects of personal finance is figuring out the stylish way to use our money. For the Millennial generation, especially, it's tough to figure out how to save big on a small budget. But, the key to lessening your spending is to cut back a little in each area, versus taking out big gobbets of your budget each at once. It may take a little work in the morning but you will find your financial stress starts to drop.

For example, you are suitable to save and pay off further of your debt.

Then are eight simple but effective ways to cut back on your charges and increase savings.

1. Put any bonuses Into Savings

There's no better feeling than seeing $20 in an old jacket fund or while you are cleaning out your car. Rather than pocketing that cash and potentially losing it at an alternate time, pay yourself first by automatically depositing it into your savings account. You can do that with larger quantities too, similar to your duty refund or a time- end perk. The same goes for your periodic rise if you get one at work. Channel the fresh amount into your 401(k) plan to grow your nest egg briskly.

2. Make Meals at Home

It can be tough to find the energy to make a mess after a long day at work. Start out with the habit of cooking at least twice a week, if you eat out frequently, and sluggishly make up to three or four times a week. However, find time on Sunday to mess up many easy feasts for the week, If that's not realistic for you. This way you will have a mess ready to go when you come home from work.

3. Make a Grocery List Before Going to the Store

If you have ever gone to the grocery store without a list or when you are empty it can be tempting to buy more food than you typically would. Pre-plan what you will need for the week before going to the store to not only make sure you do not forget anything but also to avoid picking up redundant particulars you do not need. A list helps make sure you avoid making another unnecessary trip and temptation. And, it can also help with making mess fix more affordable.

4. Set a Shopping Limit
Make it a habit to avoid buying effects on impulse. However, stay a day or two and see if you are still allowing it, If you find yourself wanting a precious fleece you stumbled upon at the boardwalk. And in the meantime, look online for printable tickets or promo canons from pasteboard apps you could apply to save money on the purchase.

5. Clean out Your Closet and Sell What You Can
As spring approaches, it may be time to go through your closet and get rid of the things you never wear. These clothes just take up redundant space and could potentially earn you some redundant cash. However, go room by room through your home looking for effects you can get rid of, If you want to go full minimalist. Once you have done some deep cleaning look into hosting a garage trade or sell some of your particulars to a consignment store.

6. Cancel Club Enrollments or Entertainment Bills
It can be easy to forget about automatically recreating yearly bills. If you have a spa class that you have always had but never used, it may be time to cancel it. Also, if you have a string but find

yourself substantially watching Netflix, see if it makes sense to cancel your string bill. Spending $100 a month on string television may not feel like a lot on a yearly basis but that is $1,200 a time you could be saving!.
Eliminating the redundant charges you infrequently use could make a significant difference in your budget.

7. Embrace DIY systems

Rather than going out to buy a new face mask, see if you can make one with the particulars you formerly have at home. Pinterest is a phenomenon tool for DIYers. Use it to find free, easy fashions for recipes, drawing hacks, and ways to use the most out of effects you have around the house.

8. Use a Budgeting App

It's easy to overspend when we are not setting limits and holding ourselves responsible. Some apps like Mint and Quicken can help you track daily, daily, or yearly spending to see where you need to cut back and admit substantiated advice grounded on your financial requirements and goals.

How To Practice Mindful Spending

Learn to master the skill of making mindful purchases and you will begin to gain the financial benefits of a strong money mindset.

Try these tips to help you appreciate your purchases, avoid impulse deals, and keep a grip on your money

1. Track it

We recommend an inspection of your spending habits to find out where you might have room to trim your purchases. Do a check- heft on your expenses daily, yearly, or yearly to cover where you can cut back. Viewing your purchases on an itemized list makes it easy to see where there's room to ameliorate. It's easy to forget about a daily trip to the coffee shop, but those takeout orders can add up!

2. Set up your budget

By establishing your financial goals, you give yourself a commodity to work towards which will outline your coming moves towards the goalpost. Choose what types of purchases are a clear " yes ", and what types of purchases are a clear " no ". Determine what you want your money to buy and establish priorities among those goals.
Get a kickstart on your budget moment by using our Budgeting Basics Workbook.

3. Designate " fun " Money

Mindful or aware spending does not mean you can not have any fun! After all, you should plan to include some fun into your goals. By setting aside a portion of your money that can be used for effects that do not align with your goals, you are not depriving yourself of a little retail way out on occasion.

4. Disable one-click buying
Set yourself up for aware spending success by killing one-click or one-swipe purchasing in your account settings. Barring the convenience of royal spending will ameliorate your chances of avoiding those impulse buys.

5. Pause before you buy.
Giving yourself a bit more time to concentrate on what you are buying will make you more purposeful about your purchase.
Give this a pass.
Take at least 10 seconds before any purchase to consider whether the purchase is perfecting or diverting from your life. Consider staying a many hours or until the following day to make significant purchases. Just like making any big decision, taking time to " sleep on it " can help you really think about the purchase and determine if it's in your stylish interest. You can ask yourself
Do I need this?
How important enjoyment or use will I gain from this purchase?
Does this align with my goals?
Can I go?
What differently could this money be used for?
The purchase may veritably well be worth making, and you may find a deeper sense of satisfaction in a purchase that you have taken the time to really

consider. Or perhaps hereafter you will realize you do not need or want it, and that money will still be in your wallet, ready to spend on a commodity you will really enjoy!

6. Ask yourself " Why "
Before you reach for your card, or click Apple Pay or PayPal, ask yourself some of the following questions:
Why am I making this purchase? Why do I want this?
Why will this purchase ameliorate my future?
Is it an impulse buy?
Is this commodity I really need?
Is this a retail remedy purchase? Am I buying it because it's on trade? Is this " a deal that's too good to pass up "?
As Manitobans, we love a good deal but try not to let the deals and deals drive your reason to buy. Relate to your budget and your goals to guide you toward success.

Benefits of Mindful Spending

These tips will help you learn how to make further mindful purchases in your life. When you become more purposeful with your money, you will start to see positive results throughout your life, in addition to having further money in your fund! We hope this process will help you   Realize what you really want and need.

1. Develop the capability to just say no to purchases that do not align with your goals
2. Learn the true value of your money
3. Pay off debt swiftly
4. Increase happiness, drop buyer's remorse
5. Support quality over volume
6. Accomplish long- term goals

Now it's up to you to take action on these tips to master your money mindset! Start by paying further attention to making mindful purchases and act by applying these practices one step at a time. With a little bit of practice, you'll negotiate getting purposeful with your money and rest easy knowing that your money is working for you, not against you, in eventually changing peace of mind with your finances. However, you can change your life! If you can flex your money mindset.

IMPULSE BUYING

Avoiding Impulse Buying in Buy and Homework

1. The Psychology Behind It (The Power of Impulse Buying)
Impulse buying is a phenomenon that affects us all at some point in our lives. It refers to the act of making unplanned purchases, constantly driven by an immediate desire or emotion, without considering the long- term consequences. While it may bring temporary satisfaction, impulse buying

can have a significant impact on our finances and overall well- being.
To more understand this behavior stop's claw into the psychology behind impulse buying.

2. Emotional triggers

MOne of the primary drivers of impulse buying is the emotional response it elicits. Advertisers and marketers are well alive of this and constantly employ various tactics to stopcock into our passions. For example, limited-time offers or flash deals produce a sense of urgency, making us feel like we might miss out if we do not act directly. Also, attractive packaging, catchy taglines, and celebrity autographs can spark positive passions and make us more likely to make impulsive purchases.

3. The pleasure principle

Impulse buying is nearly tied to the pleasure principle, which suggests that we seek immediate delectation and pleasure. When we see a commodity that catches our eye and triggers positive passions, our brain releases dopamine, a neurotransmitter associated with pleasure and price. This swell of dopamine creates a sense of anticipation and excitement, making us more susceptible to impulse buying. Retailers strategically place tempting particulars near checkout counters to subsidize this phenomenon.

4. Social Influence

The power of social influence can not be underrated when it comes to impulse buying. We are constantly told by the conduct and conduct of others, particularly in social settings. For example, if we see our buddies or associates making impulsive purchases or agitating the rearmost must- have item, we may feel compelled to do the same to fit in or avoid feeling left out. This social pressure can stamp our rational decision- making processes and lead to impulsive buying behavior.

Tips for Avoiding Impulse Buying

While impulse buying may feel hard to repel, there are strategies we can employ to regain control over our spending habits. There are also numerous tips to help you avoid falling into the impulse buying trap:

1. Make a shopping list:
Before heading to the store or browsing online, make a list of the particulars you genuinely need. Stick to this list and avoid swinging from it unless absolutely necessary.

2. Stay it out:
 When you feel the appetite to make an impulsive purchase, give yourself a cooling-off period.
Stay for at least 24 hours before making a decision. constantly, the original excitement fades, and you realize that you don't really need or want the item.

3. Track your spending:
Keep a record of your charges to gain a better understanding of your purchasing patterns. This awareness can help you identify triggers and make farther apprehensive choices.

4. Set a budget:
Establish a budget for voluntary spending and stick to it. Having a fated limit can help impulse buying and ensure that you're managing your finances responsibly.

Implementing the 50/30/20 rule for budgeting

The 50/30/20 Rule
The50/30/20 rule is a simplified budgeting system designed to help you better manage your act of spending while also stowing down finances for the future.
According to the 50/30/20 rule, you should spend:
50% of your after-tax income on must-haves
30% on wants
20% on savings and paying down debt

How to make a budget using the 50/30/20 rule

Creating a budget using the 50/30/20 rule is not a one-and-done process. You will look at your income, assess your current spending habits, set goals and also readjust your budget regularly. Then's how to get started.

1. Calculate your after-duty income
The first step to creating a 50/30/20 budget is to determine your after- duty income — how important money you bring home after covering taxes.
However, Hanson says, " You can look at your most recent hires and calculate a yearly figure, If you work a traditional job in which your employer issues hires and regularly deducts levies and Social Security. "   Still, life, or disability insurance decorations, If your employer deducts health. You will account for these costs later on in your " must-money" order.

Still, freelancer, another type of unconventional worker, If you are a contractor.
Tally over all the deposits for the month — from jobs, gigs, guests, et cetera, and also subtract the amount you need to set aside for levies. You can look to last time's duty returns for a good palpitation on this.

You should also be sure to include any supplemental income you might get, like child support, tips, commissions, and conjugal support. In the event these beget your income to change, you can add up many months of earnings to determine a rough normal.

2. Assess recent spending

Next, it's time to get a handle on your household expenditures and estimate how those fit into the 50/30/20 system.

" Review your charges from the previous month, " Hanson says. " also classify each expenditure into one of those three orders — requirements, wants and savings and debt. " It sounds easy, but you may have hundreds of charges to severance through — and some may not be easily positioned in any category.

However, then what should go under each section, according to " All Your Worth " If you need help.

Must- haves:

Housing

Utilities

Basic food needs

Phone and internet service

Medical care

Insurance

Transportation

Child care

Property levies

Legal scores, like child support or alimony

Contractual scores payment plans(spa enrollments, appliance payments,etc.)

Minimal loan payments(pupil loans, auto loans,etc.)

Savings/ debts

Monthly contributions to retirement accounts

Other savings or council account benefactions

Redundant debt payments(beyond the needed minimum payments) Wants

Eating out
Gifts
Entertainment
Streaming services
Country club dues
Massages and beauty treatments Extracurriculars and assignments Other Non-essentials
Once you have added up the last month's expenses, you can determine how important your income is going into each order — and most importantly, whether your current spending complies with the 50/30/20 rule or if you need to make adaptations. There are also calculators, like this bone from Intuit, that can help with this step.

3. Make a plan
Still, you will need to make some changes, If your current spending habits and charges do not relatively align with the 50/30/20 rule. This might include reducing your spending on " wants" or changing places to cut back on " must- have " costs, conceivably by changing your insurance plan or refinancing your mortgage.
There's an illustration
After- duty income $5,000
Must- haves $2,500(50%)
Wants $1,500(30%)
Savings $500(10%)

In the above script, you are right on target with your must-have spending, but the others are out of balance. You could look at your expenditures in the " wants " order over the last many months to determine some implicit areas to cut back on.

To insure you are not spending further than you should in each order, you can also try separating your finances into different bank accounts — one for each order,

4. Reassess regularly
At the launch of your budgeting trip, go through and classify your charges every month to ensure you are still in line with your 50/30/20 goals. " As you come more familiar and comfortable with your budget, you can check on it and rethink it.

Strategies for Budgeting for Groceries
Learning how to budget foodstuffs can assist
you spare advance to put toward
your financial claims.
Then are some ways to assist you learn how to
budget foodstuffs.

1. Track current investing
Some time recently you figure out what you ought
to be investing on nourishment, it is vital to figure
out what you are spending on nourishment.
Keep basic supply store bills to
induce a practical picture of your

current investing behavior. It might offer
assistance to break down investing by arranging
(by means of a spreadsheet or on
paper), counting potables, create, etc. Once you
have done this, you will get a thought of where you
wish to trim down your basic supply charge.
2. Distribute a chance of your wage
How imperative each household spends
on nourishment shifts based on wage and
how various individuals ought to be encouraged.
Consider utilizing budget calculator in case you 're
not beyond any doubt where to begin.
3. Dodge eating out
The information from the Bureau of
Labor Measurements appears a
13% increment in nourishment investing in the U.S.
a jump driven by
rising buys on eating out. Dodging eating out
where conceivable can offer
assistance decreases your general food spending.
However, be beyond any doubt to figure eating
down from domestic into your nourishment budget
and adhere to your restrain, In the event that you
are difficulty dating or appreciate caffs
with friends.
4. Do plan your meals
It's much easier to stay to a budget when you have
a arrange. Furthermore, having a reason for each
grocery thing you purchase may help ensure
nothing goes to squander or fair sits in your closet
unused. Do not
be insane of straightforward servings of mixed

greens or meatless Mondays not each mess needs to be a epicure involvement.

5. Keep a fridge grocery list

Keep a bewitched grocery list on your fridge so that you just supplant particulars as demanded. This may assist you purchase nourishment you know you will eat. Staying to a list within the basic need store may assist you remain responsible and not spend money on reused or valuable particulars.

6. Eat well before you go to the store

On the off chance that your mother gave you this exhortation developing up, she was onto something: concurring to considers, customers spend more when hungry. Eating before planning to the basic supply store may assist you maintain a strategic distance from tantalizing foods that can cause you to go over budget.

7. Watch out with coupons

Getting 50% off ketchup may be a bargain — unless you do not require ketchup. Be careful of coupons for things you don't need. On the off chance that the thing is not on your list, you are not sparing at all, but or maybe investing on something you do not really need.

8. Grasp the bulk section

The bulk area of your grocery store may assist you discover reasonable staples, find modern nourishments and bring assortment into your count calories. Take the time to compare the cost of prepackaged goods versus bulk — bulk is likely cheaper.

9. Bring lunch to work

Picture this: you're attempting to adhere to a nourishment budget, and one day at work you realize it's lunchtime but you overlooked packing lunch. All the feast arranging and keen shopping within the world won't offer assistance on the off chance that you do not have nourishment once you require it.

10. Cherish your leftovers

Instead of tossing your scraps absent, attempt to eat them to dodge squandering cash. To keep things curiously, hunt for ways to repurpose nourishments — yesterday's remaining taco meat can end up today's shepherd's pie.

11. Keep an inventory

Keeping a list on your fridge of what you have got hand can assist you dodge nourishment squander and get inventive when dinner arranging. And it's an awesome way to urge the foremost to utilize grocery things that are sold bigger amounts than you would like a single formula. Not sure what to do with that mammoth bunch of celery or box of spinach you have got over from another formula? Attempt out a few online formula blogs or destinations that offer formula thoughts based on some fixings you input.

12. Freezes prepared food that are going bad

Another way to dodge squandering food is to freeze or solidify things that seem like they are about to go bad. Natural products that is past their prime can be solidified or frozen and utilized in smoothies. Make twofold clumps of soups, sauces and prepared goods so you will have an option to request takeout after you do not feel like cooking.

13. Utilize curbside pickup

About 29% of shoppers conceded that seeing a thing that looked as good to pass up drove them to drive buys. Utilizing curbside pickup can offer assistance to anticipate you from obtaining spontaneous items.

14. Check the top and foot shelves

Astute basic supply stores know that eye level is where the foremost deals happen. In reality, shoppers select about 80% more items at eye level than at the foot rack. So the following time you are out shopping, take a fast see up and down — you'll discover a way better bargain covered up out of sight.

CHAPTER FOUR

Understanding the importance of an emergency fund

An emergency finance (stormy day finance) is cash that's set aside to cover the fetching of startling, and frequently costly, occasions. These reserve funds are implied to be utilized for genuine, critical needs—like to pay lease when your wage dries up or to foot a spontaneous restorative charge.

Of all the crisis finance benefits, the greatest one is that it permits you to pay for life's necessities without having to rack up an adjustment on your credit card, take out a credit, or tap into your home's equity.

An emergency finance is not an individual slush support for when your skis break or you are looking at a modern dress for your best friend's wedding. (Pleasant attempt!) Knowing when to use your crisis finance is as imperative as knowing why you wish one.

Why do I require an emergency fund

Emergency reserves make a budgetary buffer that can keep you above water in a time of need without having to depend on credit cards or high-interest advances. It can be particularly imperative to have a stormy finance in case you have got since it can assist you maintain a strategic distance from borrowing more.

When and how to utilize your emergency fund Emergency reserves can offer assistance for the charge within the occasion of startling therapeutic and dental bills, domestic and auto repairs, and work misfortunes, but they can moreover cover other unforeseen costs. For example, later a long time have seen rising costs on everything from food to gas.

Fundamentally, in the event that you think your short-term checking account is not planning to cover any basic bills or costs, such as lodging, utilities, and nourishment, at that point you ought to utilize your crisis finance. By the way, in the event that you are pondering where to keep your emergency support, consider high-yield investment funds accounts, cash showcase accounts, CDs, and IRAs. Items and administrations that are not fundamental, such as TV spilling administrations or magazine memberships, drop into the "want" category. They ought to not be paid for with emergency funds.

Benefits of Emergency Funds

Building an emergency support offers the taking after benefits:

1. Reduces stretch levels
In light of an emergency, such as a sudden work misfortune, car inconveniences, or startling domestic repairs, such frequencies without a doubt undermine one's budgetary wellness, which eventually actuates stress.
Without any sort of cushion to combat the potential occasions, people are amassing noteworthy dangers that can be hindering their day-to-day lives. Be that as it may, by building emergency finance, it gives people certainty and the capacity to overcome such unforeseen occasions without being monetarily concerned.

2. Empowers saving behaviour
By building an emergency fund, it propels people to spare and decrease the enticement of spending their cash on pointless merchandise, such as extravagances extending from TVs to video game consoles.

3. Dodges terrible debt
With emergency support, people would not have to consider utilizing terrible debt – such as high-interest credit cards – to finance their needs. Due to reckless behavior, utilizing this sort of obligation

can lead to higher installments caused by extra intrigued, expenses, and generally higher penalties.

Downsides of Emergency Funds

The downsides of keeping an crisis support incorporate the following:

1. Lower retirement savings

By including cash for emergency support, it decreases the choice of distributing any extra reserves to other programs, such as retirement investment funds or paying down a contract. Hence, crisis reserves diminish the probability of accomplishing other monetary goals.

2. Opportunity taken a toll of investing

The value of cash is worth more presently than it is within the future. By adding cash to the emergency fund, people are bringing down their chances of accepting the next return by contributing within the stock showcase and being uncovered to compound interest. In this way, crisis stores forgo the opportunity to utilize one's cash to produce more wealth.

Prioritizing Speculations or Emergency Funds

It is important to construct emergency support some time recently, wandering off to develop other sources of income streams, such as contributing in stocks. In spite of the fact that building a portfolio without a doubt yields more noteworthy long-term returns, the stock advertise itself is unstable, and returns can individually change based on financial occasions that lead to a downturn, such as a recession.

In this manner, in the event that people wish to invest with a part of their emergency fund, they may be able to do so through the following:
High-yield investment funds accounts
Cash showcase accounts
Certificates of store (CDs)

Setting up an Emergency Fund

There are two decently straightforward ways to start building up a stormy day fund:
Disseminate a settled rate of one's month to month compensation and designate it to the support. In order to do so, one must begin with calculating a guess of their three-month living costs as a target. At that point, the person can redirect a parcel of their paycheck according to how many months they would like to attain.

For example, if Jon has to $6,000 to attain months' worth of emergency funds, it can be split into $500 payments across a span of one year.

Choosing the Idealize Emergency Fund Size
The degree of your emergency fund for the most part depends on your individual circumstances and

budgetary targets. Budgetary masters by and huge recommend having three to six months' worth of living costs saved up in your emergency fund. Be that because it may, it's crucial to consider factors such as work soundness, dependents, and any advancing budgetary commitments when choosing the perfect size. For example, in case you have got relentless work and irrelevant cash related commitments, three months' worth of costs may be satisfactory. On the other hand, in case you have got dependents or work in an industry with tall work insecurity, indicating for six months or more may be advisable.

Methods for Building Your Emergency Fund

1. Cut Back on Non-Essential Costs: Start by looking into your month to month budget and recognizing locales where you will be contributing. Consider cutting back on discretionary costs such as eating out, entertainment enrollments, or shopping for non-essential things. Occupying these saves towards your emergency back will offer help to enliven its growth.

2. Robotize Your Venture stores: Set up a modified trade from your paycheck or checking account particularly into your emergency fund. By robotizing your speculation funds, you

ensure a solid commitment without the allurement to spend the cash someplacem else. Without a doubt small entireties incorporate up over time, so don't put down the control of typical, incremental savings.

3. Increase Your Pay:
On the off chance that your current wage doesn't allow for basic speculation reserves, consider examining ways to amplify your benefit. This appears to incorporate taking on a side gig, outsourcing, or in fact orchestrating a raise or progression at your current work. The extra salary can be straightforwardly designated towards your crisis finance, assisting its growth.

4. Utilize Fortunes and Rewards: When unforeseen budgetary godsends come your way, such as a year-end reward or assess discount, stand up to the allurement to rampage spend. Instep, designate a parcel or the aggregate of these godsends towards your crisis finance. This not as it were boosts your emergency finance but too makes a difference you keep up a taught approach to sparing.

Differentiating between essential and non-essential expenses

To achieve financial success, it is crucial to differentiate between essential and non-essential expenses. By understanding the distinction between these two categories, we can make thoughtful decisions about how we allocate our hard-earned money.

Here's a breakdown of essential and non-essential expenses:

1. Essential Expenses:
   These are the necessary costs for our basic needs and obligations that we must address to sustain a comfortable and functional life. They include:
   - Housing: Rent or mortgage payments, property taxes, and utility bills.
   - Food: Groceries and essential dining expenses.
   - Transportation: Commuting costs, vehicle maintenance, and insurance.
   - Health: Medical bills, insurance premiums, and necessary medications.
   - Education: Tuition fees, study materials, and necessary school-related expenses.
   - Debt Payments: Minimum payments on loans and credit card bills.
   - Insurance: Life insurance, disability insurance, and other essential coverage.
   - Taxes: Income taxes and other mandatory tax payments.

- Basic Clothing: Clothes required for day-to-day living.

2. Non-Essential Expenses:
These are the discretionary costs that enhance our quality of life but are not essential to our immediate needs. They include:

- Entertainment: Dining out, going to the movies, concerts, or other recreational activities.
- Travel: Vacations and non-essential trips.
- Hobbies: Expenses related to hobbies or personal interests.
- Luxury Items: Expensive gadgets, designer clothes, and accessories.
- Eating Out: Meals at restaurants or take-out that go beyond basic sustenance.
- Subscription Services: Non-essential subscriptions like streaming services, gym memberships, or magazine subscriptions.
- Impulse Purchases: Non-essential items bought on a whim, often driven by marketing or temporary desires.

Understanding the distinction between essential and non-essential expenses is crucial for effective budgeting and financial planning. It enables us to prioritize our spending, ensuring that the majority of our income is allocated towards fulfilling our essential needs and financial obligations. By reducing or eliminating non-essential expenses, we create opportunities to save, invest, and build a solid foundation for long-term financial success.

However, it is crucial to note that the difference between non-essential and essential expenses can be subjective and can differ from person to person. Some expenses that may be considered non-essential for one individual might be essential for another based on personal circumstances and priorities.

Ultimately, the key is to evaluate our spending habits, align our expenses with our financial goals, and make conscious choices that support our journey towards financial success. By striking a balance between essential and non-essential expenses, we can optimize our financial resources and cultivate a healthier and more sustainable relationship with money.

Strategies for saving and maintaining an emergency fund

Saving and maintaining an emergency fund is a crucial part of financial stability. Having a reserve of funds can protect you from unforeseen expenses and unexpected life events. Here are some strategies to help you save and maintain an emergency fund:

1. Create a Savings Goal: Ascertain how much you want to save for your stormy finance or fund. Aim

for at least three to six months' worth of living expenses, but adjust based on your personal circumstances.

2. Create a Budget: Track your income and expenses to identify areas where you can cut costs. Allocate a portion of your income specifically for your emergency fund. Prioritize savings by treating it as a non-negotiable expense in your budget.

3. Automate Savings: Set up automatic transfers from your paycheck or checking account to a separate savings account dedicated to your emergency fund. This ensures consistent savings and removes the temptation to spend that money elsewhere.

4. Reduce Non-Essential Expenses: Analyze your discretionary spending and identify areas where you can reduce expenses. Cut back on unnecessary expenses such as eating out, entertainment, or excessive shopping. Redirect those savings towards your emergency fund.

5. Save Windfall Money: Whenever you receive unexpected income like tax refunds, work bonuses, or monetary gifts, resist the urge to splurge. Instead, allocate a portion or all of it to your emergency fund.

6. Track and Control Impulse Purchases: Be mindful of impulsive buying habits. Before buying

anything, ask yourself if it is important to make the purchase or if it is confirmity with your financial goals. Delaying gratification can significantly boost your savings.

7. Explore Ways to Increase Income: Seek opportunities to increase your income through a side hustle, freelance work, or a part-time job. The additional income earned can be directly allocated towards your emergency fund.

8. Evaluate Subscriptions and Services: Regularly review your subscriptions, such as memberships or streaming services. Cancel those that you no longer use or consider unnecessary. Redirect the funds towards your emergency savings.

9. Build a Cash Cushion First: Prioritize accumulating a small cash cushion to cover immediate emergencies before focusing on long-term investments. This helps avoid going into debt for unexpected expenses.

10. Avoid Co-mingling Funds: Keep your emergency fund separate from your regular savings to prevent accidental spending. Opt for a high-yield savings account that offers some interest but is easily accessible when needed.

11. Renew the Fund: In case you need to dip into your emergency fund, make it a priority to refill the withdrawn amount as soon as possible to avoid a

deficit. Resume contributions until your fund reaches its desired level.

Note, creating and maintaining an emergency finance requires discipline, but the peace of mind it provides is inestimable. Start with small, achievable goals and gradually increase your contributions. Consistency is key to long-term financial stability.

Tips for managing unexpected financial situations

Managing unexpected financial situations can be challenging, but with the right strategies, you can navigate through them more effectively. Here are some tips to help you manage unexpected financial situations:

1. Assess the Situation: Take a step back and evaluate the extent of the financial problem. Determine the cause, urgency, and potential impact it may have on your overall financial situation.

2. Create a Plan: Develop a plan of action to address the situation. Break it down into smaller, manageable steps. Consider short-term solutions like negotiating payment plans, seeking financial assistance, or finding ways to increase your income temporarily.

3. Prioritizing Expenditures: Be able to differentiate between essential and non-essential expenses.

Prioritize basic necessities such as food, shelter, utilities, and transportation. Cut back on non-essential expenses until you regain financial stability.

4. Communicate with Creditors: If you're struggling to meet your financial obligations, communicate with your creditors promptly. Many lenders and service providers are willing to work out alternative payment arrangements or provide temporary relief options.

5. Seek Professional Advice: If you're overwhelmed or uncertain about how to handle the situation, don't hesitate to consult with a financial advisor or counselor. They can provide guidance and help you develop a tailored plan based on your situation.

6. Build a Support Network: Reach out to friends, family, and local community organizations for support. They may provide valuable advice, emotional support, or even resources to help you get through the financial crisis.

7. Cut Back on Discretionary Spending: Temporarily reduce or eliminate non-essential expenses, such as dining out, entertainment, or subscriptions. Redirect those funds towards necessary expenses or your emergency savings.

8. Explore Additional Income Sources: Look for opportunities to earn extra income. Consider

freelancing, part-time jobs, or gig economy work that can help bridge the financial gap during difficult times.

9. Review Insurance Coverage: Assess your insurance policies to ensure they provide adequate protection. Health insurance, car insurance, and home insurance can offer a safety net during unexpected events that may lead to financial strain.

10. Avoid Taking on More Debt: While it may be tempting, try to avoid taking on additional debt to solve the immediate problem. Taking on more financial obligations can exacerbate the situation in the long run.

11. Take Care of Your Well-being: Unexpected financial situations can be stressful. Take care of yourself physically and emotionally. Practice self-care, seek support from loved ones, and adopt stress management techniques.

Remember, unexpected financial situations can be temporary hurdles. By remaining calm, proactive, and resourceful, you can effectively manage these challenges and regain financial stability.

CHAPTER FIVE

Paying Off Debt

Understanding different types of debt and their implications

All debts are not made up. By and large, there are two primary sorts of debt are:
1. Secured debt
2. Unsecured debt

Inside these sorts, you will see spinning and installment debt. Aside from the fact that they merely owe cash, these sorts of debt are diverse. For occasion, your contract is an example of secured obligation, whereas a case of unsecured debt is your credit card. How best to handle each kind of obligation varies.

SECURED DEBT

When you put up collateral for a credit, you're managing with a secured debt. For example, a contract is regularly secured by your domestic and an auto credit is more often than not secured by your car.

On the off chance that you get as well distant behind on paying a secured obligation, the loan specialist can seize the debt—foreclose on your domestic or repossess your car, for example.

If the seized collateral does not cover the debt you owe, the lender may go after you in court to gather the rest of the money.

For occurrence, in the event that you owe $10,000 on your car, but it's valued at a fair $6,000, the bank may look for a court judgment against you to urge the contrast ($4,000).

Other types of secured debt are: a home equity loan and a home equity line of credit (HELOC).. In both cases, the obligation is secured by your home.

Merits of Secured Debt

Potential focal points of secured debt include:
1. You will be able to borrow a significant sum of cash.
Why? Since the moneylender knows they will get their cash back, either by collecting your advance installments or by seizing your property in case you drop behind on your credit payments.
2. You will score a lower intrigued rate since a secured credit includes less chance to the lender than other sorts of debt, such as unsecured debt.
3. You will qualify for an yearly charge finding on the intrigued paid on a few secured advances, such as a contract or home value loan.

Demerits of Secured Debt

Potential impediments of secured obligation include:

1. You will be able to own property, such as a domestic or car, that secures the credit in the event that you come up short to create your payments.

2.You are ordinarily borrowing cash for a particular thing, like a domestic or car, instead of being able to utilize the money for an assortment of purposes, as you will with an individual loan.

How Best To Handle Secured Debt

Here are four tips to maintain a strategic distance from inconvenience with secured debt:
1. Continuously make your credit installments on time and pay at least the minimum sum due.
2. Let your moneylender know in case you are battling to keep up with the payments.
3. Offer your property in case required. For example, in the event that the moneylender is getting prepared to repossess your car, consider offering it and paying off the debt. This could assist you maintain a strategic distance from the fetch related to repossession and anticipate a negative stamp from appearing up on your credit report.
4. Reach out to your bank on the off chance that you are having inconvenience making installments. For example, in case you are not able to create a contract installment, contact your loan specialist right absent. The moneylender may decrease your installments for a brief time or put them on hold so you can capture up on your debt. Or the bank may

indeed alter the credit terms to lower the month to month payment.

UNSECURED DEBT

Unlike secured obligation, unsecured obligation is not supported by any resource such as a domestic or car. Instead, a bank allow you to borrow cash based on your creditworthiness (seen capacity to reimburse the debt).

Common sorts of unsecured obligation include:

Most credit cards

Medical bills

Most individual loans

Understudy loans

Since unsecured obligation is not sponsored by an asset, a bank can not seize your property in the event that you fail to form installments. But in the event that you fall flat to make installments for as long, the creditor likely will report the missed installments to the major credit bureaus. In addition, the lender may turn your debt over to a debt collector or look for a court judgment requiring you to pay the debt.

Merits of Unsecured Debt

Potential advantages of unsecured debt include:

1. You do not have to be property, such as a car or domestic, to get an unsecured credit or unsecured credit card.

2. Your unsecured obligation is not sponsored by collateral, which implies a leaser can not seize your

property in the event that you come up short to pay, without taking legitimate action.

3. Your application for an unsecured credit or credit card may be endorsed more rapidly than an application for a secured credit since these advances don't require collateral.

Demerits of Unsecured Debt

Potential drawbacks of unsecured debt include:

1. You will regularly be charged higher intrigued rates for unsecured obligation than for secured obligation. Moneylenders take a more prominent financial risk with unsecured debt and have no collateral to seize if you fail to create payments.

2. It will be more difficult to qualify for an unsecured loan or credit card if you do not have a solid credit history.

How Best To Handle Unsecured Debt

Here are one or tips for avoiding trouble with unsecured debt or getting out of trouble:

1. Always make your payments on time and pay at least the minimum amount due.
2. Reach out to creditors if you've gotten behind on payments. He or she may be willing or planning on repayment.

Revolving or Spinning debt

Revolving debt can be unsecured or secured. Credit cards are a case of unsecured spinning obligation. Domestic value lines of credit (HELOCs) are a case of secured rotating debt. A debt account comes with a credit restriction set by the lender. With rotating credit, you will borrow against the credit constraints over an inconclusive period. The sum of accessible credit diminishes as you make buys and rises as you make installments. The least sum due each month varies based on the adjusted amount.

How Best To Handle Revolving Debt

Here are three tips for dodging inconvenience with revolving debt or getting out of trouble:
1. Observe your spending.
2. Pay in full each month.
In the event that you can not, attempt to pay more than the least sum due each month and make each installment some time recently the due date.
3. If you are having trouble paying back your debt, handle higher-interest debt some time recently lower-interest debt. Known as the debt torrential slide strategy, over the long run, this may assist you to spare cash on intrigued charges.

INSTALLMENT DEBT

Installment debt is another term for non-revolving debt. Intallment debt refers to an advance that gives a lump-sum sum of cash at the beginning of the advance. For example, you might take out a $10,000 individual loan to solidify existing debt. Each month, you pay a set sum of cash (like $300), which cash is paid over a set period (like 36 months). These sorts of loan can be secured or unsecured.

Sorts of installment advances include:

Mortgages
Auto loans
Understudy loans
Individual loans

How Best To Handle Installment Debt

Here are five tips for dodging inconvenience with installment (non-revolving) debt or getting out of trouble:

1. Pay on time, each time, and pay in full
2. Make installments each week instead of once a month. By doing this, you will be able the sum of time it takes to pay off the loan and diminish the sum of intrigued you pay.
3. Pay more cash each month. You will be able off an installment advance more rapidly by cushioning your month to month installment. For instance, on the off chance that you have got a car advance with a month to month installment of $250, you might

tack on another $50 to bring each installment to $300.

4. Make one additional installment each year. In case you do not feel comfortable making installments each other week or bumping up the sum of each monthly payment, consider making one additional installment each year. This may diminish the length of the advance and can diminish the sum of intrigued you pay.

5. Renegotiate the advance. In case you can score a lower intrigued rate, consider renegotiating the credit to recoil the length of the advance and shrivel the sum of intrigued you pay.

Having Trouble Paying Debt

Consider Debt Relief

In case you are having inconvenience paying your debt and your banks won't create a reimbursement arrangement for you, consider reaching a credit counseling organization or another debt alleviation organization. A credit counseling service can, for example, assist you make a budget and come up with other arrangements for your obligation issues.

Debt Management

One of those check might be a debt administration arrangement. Beneath one of these plans, a credit counseling organization creates a installment course of action in conjunction with unsecured banks. These banks regularly concur to ease your monetary burden by bringing down your intrigued rate or postponing expenses. With a debt administration arrange, you make month to month installments to the credit counseling office, which at that point divides that cash among your unsecured creditors.

Debt Settlement
Another road for adapting with a heap of unsecured obligation is to enroll offer assistance from a for-profit debt settlement program. In any case, typically an exorbitant and hazardous elective that is for the most part and choice of final resort. These companies arrange with lenders to settle your debt with a lump-sum installment that's less than what you owe.

To make the lump-sum installment, you set aside a certain sum each month. That cash is exchanged into an account that develops until there's sufficient cash to pay the settled debt. Be beyond any doubt that these programs as often as possible tell their clients to halt making month to month installments specifically to unsecured lenders, which can cause a negative check on your credit. Furthermore, you might end up being charged late expenses and punishments by those lenders.

Strategies for effective debt repayment

Effective debt repayment strategies are essential for individuals looking to regain financial stability and improve their overall financial well-being. Here are several strategies to consider:

1. Assess Your Debt Situation: Begin by compiling a comprehensive list of all your debts, including balances, interest rates, and minimum monthly payments. This overview will help you prioritize which debts to focus on first.

2. Create a Budget: Establish a realistic budget that accounts for all your expenses, including debt payments. Allocate as much of your income as possible towards debt repayment while still ensuring you have enough for essentials like housing, utilities, groceries, and transportation.

3. Prioritize High-Interest Debts: Target debts with the highest interest rates first. By paying off these debts more quickly, you'll reduce the amount of interest you accrue over time, ultimately saving money in the long run.

4. Utilize the Debt Snowball Method: With this approach, you focus on paying off the smallest debts first while making minimum payments on larger debts. Once the smallest debt is paid off, you roll that payment into the next smallest debt, creating a snowball effect that accelerates debt repayment.

5. Consider the Debt Avalanche Method: This method involves prioritizing debts with the highest interest rates regardless of balance size. By

tackling high-interest debts first, you minimize the total amount paid in interest over time.

6. Negotiate Lower Interest Rates: Contact your creditors to inquire about lowering your interest rates. Many creditors are willing to negotiate, especially if you have a history of on-time payments or are facing financial hardship.

7. Consolidate or Refinance: Consolidating multiple debts into a single loan or refinancing existing loans to secure a lower interest rate can simplify repayment and potentially reduce overall interest costs.

8. Increase Your Income: Explore opportunities to boost your income through side gigs, freelance work, overtime hours, or seeking higher-paying employment. Allocating additional funds towards debt repayment can accelerate your progress.

9. Cut Expenses: Identify areas where you can cut discretionary spending and redirect those funds towards debt repayment. This may involve dining out less frequently, canceling subscription services, or finding cheaper alternatives for everyday expenses.

10. Stay Motivated and Persistent: Debt repayment requires discipline and perseverance. Celebrate small victories along the way, such as paying off a credit card or reaching a milestone in your repayment plan. Keep your long-term financial goals in mind to stay motivated during challenging times.

11. Seek Professional Assistance if Needed: If you're struggling to manage your debt on your own,

consider seeking guidance from a financial counselor or debt management agency. These professionals can provide personalized advice and assistance in developing a repayment plan tailored to your unique situation.

12. Avoid Accumulating New Debt: While focusing on repaying existing debts, make a conscious effort to avoid accumulating new debt. Cut up credit cards if necessary and practice responsible spending habits to prevent further financial strain.

By implementing these strategies and remaining committed to your debt repayment goals, you can take control of your finances and work towards a debt-free future.

Prioritizing debts based on interest rates and balances

Prioritizing debts based on interest rates and balances can be a smart strategy to focus on paying off high-cost debts more efficiently. Here's how you can prioritize your debts:

1. Enumerate Your Debts: Make a list of all your debts, including credit cards, loans, and other outstanding balances. Note down the interest rates and outstanding balances for each debt.

2. Identify High-Interest Debts: Sort your debts based on their interest rates from highest to lowest. Typically, high-interest debts, such as credit card

debts, should be your priority as they accrue more interest over time.

3. Pay Minimum Payments: Make sure to pay at least the minimum payment for all your debts to avoid penalties or late fees.

4. Focus on High-Interest Debts: Allocate extra funds towards the debt with the highest interest rate while paying the minimums on other debts. This approach helps reduce the total interest you'll pay in the long run.

5. Consider Balance Transfer or Debt Consolidation: If feasible, explore options like balance transfers or debt consolidation loans. These strategies can help consolidate high-interest debts into a single lower-interest payment, making it easier to manage and pay off your debts faster.

6. Snowball or Avalanche Methods: Choose a debt repayment strategy that aligns with your financial situation and preferences. The snowball method involves paying off the smallest balance first, while the avalanche method focuses on the highest-interest debt first. Both methods have their advantages, so opt for the one that motivates you and suits your financial goals.

7. Review and Adjust: Regularly review your progress and adjust your payment strategy as

needed. As you pay off one debt, direct the freed-up funds towards the next highest priority debt.

8. Build Emergency Savings: While focusing on debt repayment, it's crucial to set aside some funds for emergencies. Having an emergency savings cushion can prevent you from accumulating more debt when unexpected expenses arise.

Remember, prioritizing debts based on interest rates and balances can help you save money on interest payments and pay off your debts faster. However, it's essential to maintain consistency, discipline, and stay committed to your debt repayment plan until you achieve your financial goals.

Exploring debt consolidation options

When exploring debt consolidation options, there are a few strategies to consider:
1. Personal Loan: One option is to obtain a personal loan from a bank or online lender. This loan could be used to pay off multiple debts, such as credit card balances or medical bills. With a personal loan, you'll have a fixed interest rate and a set repayment period.

2. Balance Transfer Credit Card: If you have significant credit card debt, transferring balances to a credit card with a low or 0% introductory APR can be an option. This allows you to consolidate your

credit card debts into one payment with potentially lower interest. However, be aware of any balance transfer fees and the duration of the introductory APR period.

3. Home Equity Loan or HELOC: If you own a home, you may be able to use the equity you've built to consolidate your debts. A home equity loan provides a lump sum of money, whereas a home equity line of credit (HELOC) allows you to borrow against your equity as needed. These options often have lower interest rates but require your home as collateral.

4. Debt Management Plan (DMP): A DMP is a program offered by nonprofit credit counseling agencies. They work with your creditors to negotiate lower interest rates and consolidate your debts into one monthly payment. DMPs typically have a set repayment period, and you make payments to the credit counseling agency, who distributes them to your creditors.

5. Debt Consolidation Company: There are companies that specialize in debt consolidation. They negotiate with your creditors to potentially lower your interest rates and create a consolidated payment plan. It's important to research and choose a reputable company, as some may charge high fees or engage in predatory practices.

Before deciding on a debt consolidation option, consider the following:

1. Evaluate your credit score and financial situation to determine eligibility and affordability.

2. Consider the interest rates, fees, and repayment terms of each option.

3. Understand the impact on your credit score and any potential risks, such as using your home as collateral.

4. Create a budget to ensure you can afford the consolidated payment.

5. Seek advice from a financial advisor or credit counselor to assess the best option for your specific circumstances.

Tips for negotiating with creditors and managing debt stress

When negotiating with creditors and managing debt stress, consider the following tips:

1. Communicate: Open communication with your creditors is key. If you're struggling to make payments, reach out to them as soon as possible and explain your situation. They may be willing to work with you to create a more manageable repayment plan.

2. Understand your rights: Familiarize yourself with the laws and regulations surrounding debt collection practices. This can help you better navigate conversations with creditors and ensure your rights are protected.

3. Prepare a budget: Develop a realistic budget that outlines your income, expenses, and debt payments. This will help you gain a better understanding of your financial picture and identify areas where you can cut costs or allocate more funds toward debt repayment.

4. Prioritizing of debts: Determine which debts are the most urgent and prioritizing them accordingly. Focus on paying off high-interest debts first, as they can accumulate more interest over time and become more difficult to manage.

5. Exploring the debt relief options: Research debt relief programs, such as debt settlement or debt consolidation. These options can help you negotiate with creditors to potentially reduce the amount owed or create a more manageable repayment plan.

6. Seek professional help: Consider working with a credit counselor or financial advisor who can offer guidance on managing your debts. They can help you create a personalized debt management plan and provide valuable resources and support.

7. Take care of your mental well-being or health: Debt stress can be overwhelming, so it's important to prioritize self-care. Find healthy outlets for stress, such as exercise, meditation or talking to a supportive friend or family member. Consider seeking professional help if you're experiencing severe anxiety or depression related to your debts.

8. Avoid accumulating debt: While managing the current debts, it's important to avoid additional debt. Try to resist the urge to rely on credit cards or loans

CHAPTER SIX

Maximizing Income Potential

Assessing current income streams and identifying opportunities for growth

Assessing your current income streams and identifying opportunities for growth is an important step in building financial stability and achieving your long-term financial goals. By understanding where your money is coming from and exploring ways and methods to multiply your income, you can create a more secure financial future. Below are some key aspects to take whilen evaluating your income streams and seeking opportunities for growth:

Assessing Current Income Streams

1. Basic Income: Start by examining your primary source of income, such as your salary from a job or earnings from a business. Calculate your net income after taxes and deductions to have a clear understanding of how much you are earning each month.

2. Secondary Income: Consider any additional sources of income you may have, such as freelance work, rental properties, investment dividends, or part-time gigs. Evaluate how much these additional income streams contribute to your overall financial picture.

3. Irregular Income: If your income fluctuates or is irregular, take the time to assess the patterns and variability. Understanding the seasonality or volatility of your income can help you better plan and manage your finances.

4. Dormant Income: Identify any sources of passive income, such as royalties, interest from investments, or rental income. Passive income can provide a steady stream of money with minimal ongoing effort, so it's important to leverage these opportunities.

5. Benefits and Perks: Consider non-monetary benefits and perks offered by your employer, such as healthcare benefits, retirement contributions, or stock options. These benefits can significantly contribute to your overall compensation package.

Identifying Opportunities for Growth

1. Skills and Expertise: Evaluate your skills, knowledge, and expertise to identify areas where you can potentially increase your income. Consider pursuing additional training, certifications, or advanced degrees to enhance your earning potential in your current field or explore new career opportunities.

2. Side Hustles and Freelancing: Explore opportunities for side hustles or freelance work that

align with your interests and skills. Utilize online platforms to market your services or products, and consider turning your hobbies into income-generating ventures.

3. Investments: Consider investing in assets that have the potential to generate passive income, such as rental properties, dividend-paying stocks, or peer-to-peer lending. Diversifying your investment portfolio can help you grow your wealth over time.

4. Entrepreneurship: If you have a business idea or passion project, consider starting your own business to generate additional income. Research market opportunities, create a business plan, and explore funding options to launch and scale your venture.

5. Negotiation and Advancement: Advocate for yourself in the workplace by negotiating salary increases, promotions, or bonuses based on your performance and contributions. Seek opportunities for advancement within your current organization or consider transitioning to a higher-paying position elsewhere.

6. Financial Literacy: Invest in your financial literacy and education to make informed decisions about income-generating opportunities. Stay updated on market trends, investment strategies, and personal

finance best practices to maximize your earning potential.L

Monitoring and Reviewing Progress

1. Track Income Sources: Keep a record of your various income streams and monitor any changes or fluctuations over time. Use budgeting tools or financial software to automate income tracking and gain insights into your earnings.

2. Regular Evaluation: Set aside time periodically to review your income sources and assess their performance. Identify opportunities for optimization, expansion, or diversification to ensure a balanced and sustainable income portfolio.

3. Goal Setting: Establish specific financial goals related to income growth and track your progress towards achieving them. Regularly reassess your goals, adjust strategies as needed, and celebrate milestones along the way.

By assessing your current income streams and proactively seeking opportunities for growth, you can cultivate a diverse and robust financial foundation. Note to stay informed, adapt to changing circumstances, and leverage your skills and resources to maximize your earning potential and achieve your long-term financial objectives.

Strategies for salary negotiations and professional advancement

Strategies for salary negotiations

1. Inquire about industry benchmarks:
Some time recently entering into a compensation transaction, investigate what other professionals in your industry are gaining. This could assist you set reasonable desires for your compensation and give proof to back up your ask.

2. Know your worth:
Determine your abilities, encounter, and all your achievements to decide your showcase esteem. This may assist you get what you bring to the table and negotiate for a better compensation that reflects your contributions.

3. Be certain:
Believe in yourself and your abilities. Approach the transaction with certainty and emphaticness, whereas still being aware and professional.

4. Do not be the first to title a number:
If possible, let the boss make the primary offer. This will assist you dodge securing inclination, which can work against you on the off chance that your starting ask is as well tall or as well low.

5. Focus on add up to stipend: Consider not as it were your base compensation, but too benefits,

rewards, stock choices, and other advantages. These can all include up to a critical portion of your compensation.

6. Highlight your esteem suggestion: Be arranged to express how you are, doing will include esteem to the company and contribute to its foot line. This will offer assistance to legitimize your compensation and point out your worth.

7. Be adaptable:
Consider elective shapes of stipend on the off chance that the boss can't meet your compensation ask. For case, you may arrange for a more adaptable plan, extra offers, or extra proficient advancement opportunities.

8. Do not burn bridges:
Indeed in the event that the arrangement doesn't result in the salary you trusted for, it's vital to preserve a positive relationship with the manager. Express appreciation for the opportunity and keep the lines of communication open for future openings. At this point, and on the off chance that it hasn't been clarified, inquire what they would be trying to find your execution to warrant an increase.

9. Practice active listening:

Pay attention to what the boss is saying and react mindfully. This may help build affinity and set up a collaborative negotiation process.

10. Get it in composing:
Once an agreement has been come to, make sure to induce the points of interest in composing. This will offer assistance to dodge mistaken assumptions or miscommunications afterward on.

Strategies for professional advancement

Some transaction aptitudes to boost your career
1. Figuring out what you need. Make a list of what is critical to you and set your needs ahead of time. You ought to enter a transaction with clear objectives and get ready to alter your desires amid this give-and-take process.

2. Make an inquiry. Is it an advancement or a distant better bundle you are centered on? You will be able to support your position by supporting it with current advertised information from the Salary Guide, such as how much workers gain in comparative positions, businesses and geographic districts.

3. Centering on the esteem you bring. You were hired for a reason, and knowing your worth can donate you the certainty to effectively arrange for a career headway. Calculate your potential commitment by appearing how you will be able to

increase the company benefits or lower costs. Construct your case with a list of your special and transferrable abilities, industry encounter, awards, and authority and collaboration capabilities. If you are in an entry-level position, you will have classes, internships or mentorship encounters you will utilize to highlight your accomplishments and skills.

4. Practicing and role-playing some time recently you arrange. The key is to induce yourself in a sure mentality. Compile a list of talking focuses so you'll convey a compelling contention for what you need. It may offer assistance to practice the discussion with a guide and to assume you're arranging for a friend.

5. Being humble, self-assured and viable. Inquire, or maybe than request. Express your suppositions whereas regarding the other side's points of view. Take a fact-driven approach to transaction. Survey your work depiction and consider anything additional you've done outside of your list of obligations, such as cutting costs or including the company culture.

6. Illustrating dynamic tuning in abilities. We have two ears and one mouth for a reason, and you should make an effort to urge the other individual to talk so you will be able to as much as possible. To fortify your interest in what the speaker has been saying and to assemble valuable data, inquire pertinent questions. A few cases incorporate, "What

administration openings seem to develop from this role?";
"What has made somebody effective in this job";
and "How do you see my part evolving?"
Tuning in isn't just valuable for lifting a discussion; it's too recognized as a profitable ability set that companies and enlisting directors are looking for.

7. Strategizing what to arrange past compensation. Be arranged to talk about points that are important to you, such as a marking or retention reward, adaptable work plan, inaccessible vs. crossbreed vs. onsite work, paid take off, childcare and educational cost repayment, your job title, upward portability choices, and the scope of work you are performing. Survey your strengths and shortcomings to arrange a practical course of activity. Too, utilize this technique: Inquire for more than you need to give yourself a few squirm room; it never hurts to begin a bit higher, particularly in this market.

8. Realizing the discussion doesn't come to a conclusion with the arranged offer. A few individuals depict this as the never-take-the-first-offer approach. You will discover it fitting to conduct a momentary circular of arrangements in case the offer wasn't what you were trusting for.

9. Knowing your bartering control. Whether you are a work candidate at your second meet or a worker seeking out for more, you should know that the

company has as of now invested in you. And, in today's work showcase, laborers are feeling progressively enabled. Are you looking for more adaptability?

The manager may be, as well. And indeed on the off chance that not, a tight labor advertisement with a deficiency of gifted experts can make managers more open to concessions when they are battling with staffing and worker retention.

10. Seeing rejection as an opportunity to memorize. Your negotiation shows your emphaticness, which is an in-demand aptitude within the working environment. Indeed, on the off chance that you do not get what you inquire for, it's likely this involvement has instructed you something almost yourself and the company, and around what you might do differently the another time, all of which are positive results.

Exploring side hustle ideas and passive income sources

Exploring side hustle ideas and passive income sources can provide you with additional streams of income to supplement your primary earnings. Consider your interests, skills, and resources to identify opportunities that align with your goals and can contribute to your financial well-being in the long run. Experiment with different ideas, track your progress, and continue refining your strategies to maximize your earning potential and achieve financial success.

The following are the side hustles ideas you can engage in to generate multiple source of income:

1. Freelance Writing/Editing: Offer your writing or editing services on freelance platforms or to businesses in need of content creation. Writing and self-publishing an ebook allows you to earn secondary income from book sales. It is a nice side hustle if you have experience or expertise on a particular subject, enjoy writing, and can market your book to reach a wider audience.

2. Virtual Assistant Services: Provide administrative support, pro bono, email management, scheduling, social media manager and other activities for individuals or businesses remotely.

3. Handmade Crafts or Art: Sell your upcycle arts, handmade crafts, images, artwork, or jewelry on online marketplaces or at local craft fairs.

4. Tutoring or Teaching: Offer tutoring services in subjects you excel in or teach skills such as blockchain, music, UX/UI design, languages, or coding.

5. Photography Services: Capture events, portraits, or stock photos for clients or sell your images to stock photography websites. If you have photography or graphic design skills, creating and

selling photos or graphic design can generate secondary income. It is a nice side hustle because it allows you to monetize your creative skills, earn royalties or commission on each sale, and have the potential for recurring income.

6. Consulting Services: Share your expertise in areas like marketing, business strategy, finance, or career development with clients seeking guidance.

7. Social Media Management: Help businesses or individuals manage their social media accounts, create content, and engage with their audience.

8. Personal Training or Fitness Coaching: Offer personalized workout plans, coaching sessions, or wellness advice to clients looking to improve their health and fitness.

9. Home Organizing Services: Assist clients in decluttering, organizing, and optimizing their living spaces for better efficiency and productivity.

10. E-commerce Store: Building and running an e-commerce store, whether through dropshipping or selling your own products, can provide secondary income. It is a nice side hustle because it allows you to tap into the growing online shopping trend, reach a wide customer base, and automate certain aspects of the business.

Start an online store selling products you create or source from suppliers, utilizing platforms like Shopify or Etsy.

11. Start a YouTube Channel:
Creating and growing a YouTube channel can bring you an alternative income through ad revenue or sponsorships. It is a great side hustle if you enjoy creating video content, have the experience or a unique perspective to share, and can frequently produce fascinating videos to attract viewers.

12. Buy and Sell Domain Names:
Buying and selling domain names, otherwise known as domain flipping, can yield passive income through profitable domain sales. It is not a bad side hustle if you have experience of market trends and can identify valuable domains.

Passive Income Sources:

1. Dividend-Paying Stocks: Invest in companies that pay regular dividends to shareholders, providing you with a passive income stream from your investments.

2. Rental Properties:Investing in real estate and renting out properties can give a steady stream of secondary sources of income through rental payments. It is a nice side hustle because it offers long-term wealth accumulation, potential tax benefits, and property value appreciation. Purchase

real estate properties to rent out to tenants, generating rental income while building equity in the property.

3. Peer-to-Peer Lending: Lend money to individuals or businesses through peer-to-peer lending platforms, earning interest on your loan investments.

4. Digital Products: Create and sell digital products such as e-books, online courses, or software that can generate passive income through sales or subscriptions.

5. Affiliate Marketing: Promote products or services through affiliate links on your website, blog, or social media channels, earning commissions for sales or leads generated. It is a good side hustle because you can choose products that align with your interests or expertise, leverage your online presence, and earn income by recommending products to your audience.

6. Royalties: Earn royalties from intellectual property such as books, music, patents, or trademarks by licensing or selling rights to use your creations.

7. Dropshipping: Start an online store without holding inventory by partnering with suppliers who fulfill orders directly to customers, earning a profit margin on each sale.

8. Automated Online Businesses: Develop automated online businesses, such as membership sites, software as a service (SaaS), or digital downloads that generate income with minimal ongoing work.

9. Real Estate Crowdfunding: Invest in real estate projects through crowdfunding platforms, pooling resources with other investors to earn returns on real estate investments.

10. Mobile Apps: Create and monetize mobile mobile apps can provide another source of income through app downloads, in-app purchases, or advertising revenue, premium subscriptions, generating passive income from app users.
It is a good side hustle if you have programming skills and can develop useful or entertaining apps that resonate with users.

11. Start a Blog and Monetize It:
Creating a successful blog and monetizing it through advertising networks or sponsored content can yield passive income. It is a nice side hustle due to the fact that it allows you to share your passion or experience, build online buyers, and earn income from ad placements or sponsored collaborations.

12. Invest in Cryptocurrency:
Investing in cryptocurrencies like Bitcoin, USDT or Ethereum can bring secondary income through price appreciation or staking rewards. It is a great side hustle if you have the experience of the cryptocurrency market, can bear the risks involve, and can stay updated with market trends and developments.

Tips for building a personal brand and expanding your network

Building a strong personal brand and expanding your network are essential for establishing your presence in your industry, attracting opportunities, and fostering meaningful connections with professionals in your field. By consistently showcasing your expertise, engaging with your audience, and actively expanding your network, you can strengthen your personal brand and unlock new opportunities for growth and success.
The following are the tips are useful:
1. Define Your Mission and Values: Clearly embrace what you stand for, your knowledge and skills, and the value you provide to your audience or clients.

2. Develop Consistent Branding: Create a cohesive brand image across all platforms, including your website, social media profiles, business cards, and other marketing materials.

3. Share Valuable Content: Create and share content that showcases your expertise, skills, and unique perspective to create yourself as an authority in your field.

4. Engage with Your Audience: React to comments, messages, and inquiries from your followers to build relationships and foster a sense of community around your brand.

5. Partner with Others: Collaborate with influencers, brands, or other professionals in your industry to increase your reach and credibility through collaborations and guest appearances.

6. Seek Feedback and Listen to Your Audience: Solicit feedback from your audience, clients, or peers to continuously ameliorate and tailor your brand messaging and offerings to their demands.

7. Participate in Networking Events: Attend industry conferences, workshops, seminars, and networking events to meet like-minded individuals, potential clients, and collaborators.

8. Utilize Social Media: Leverage social media platforms such as LinkedIn, Twitter, Instagram, or Facebook to share updates, connect with industry professionals, and display your knowledge.

9. Create a Professional Website: Build a professional website that displays your portfolio,

services, testimonials, and contact information to serve as the central hub for your personal brand.

10. Stand Authentic and Genuine: Be real and true to yourself, your values in all your interactions to create trust and credibility with your audience.

Tips for Expanding Your Network:

1. Participate in Industry Events: Attend in conferences, trade shows, meetups and industry events to meet new connections and expand your professional network.

2. Enjoin Professional Associations: Become a member of industry-specific associations or membership to connect with professionals in your field or career and to keep you abreast of the latest in the industry trends and opportunities.

3. Utilize LinkedIn: Optimize your LinkedIn profile, join and follow relevant groups, share content, and connect with professionals in your industry to expand your network, visibility and net worth.

4. Offer to Help Others: Be generous with your time, knowledge, and resources to support and assist both juniors and seniors in your network, building goodwill and embracing long-term relationships.

5. Participate in Networking Workshops: Attend networking workshops or seminars to improve your networking skills, learn effective strategies, and build confidence in connecting with others.

6. Utilize Online Platforms: Use online networking platforms such as Facebook, Meetup, Telegram, Eventbrite, or industry-specific forums to find networking events, workshops, and groups in your area.

7. Ask for Introductions: Request introductions from mutual connections or colleagues to meet new professionals and expand your network via personal referrals.

8. Follow Up and Stay Connected: After creating a new network, follow up with a personalized message, connect on social media, and maintain the relationship to create a robust network over time.

9. Host Events or Workshops: Organize your own networking events, workshops, or webinars to bring together professionals in your industry and provide value to your network.

10. Seek Mentorship: Find mentors or advisors in your field who can provide mentorship, guidance, counseling, support, and valuable insights to help you grow personally and professionally.

Leveraging skills and talents to increase income potential

There are many ways to use your skills and expertise to earn higher income. Here are some ideas:

• Distinguish high-demand skills: Inquire about the work showcase to decide which abilities are in tall demand in your industry. Consider taking courses or getting certifications to enhance your abilities and make yourself more marketable.

• Inquire for a raise: On the off chance that you accept you are coming up short on the esteem you bring to your company, it may be time to inquire for a raise. Prepare a list of your achievements and contributions to the company, and be arranged to create a case for why you merit a better salary.

• Independent or consult: If you have got abilities, you will be able to gain more cash by outsourcing or counseling. You will be able to sell your services to companies in your industry or work with some clients.

• Begin a side hustle: In the event that you have got energy or expertise exterior of your current work, consider beginning a side hustle. This may be an extraordinary way to gain additional pay whereas doing something you enjoy.

Search for higher-paying work openings: On the off chance that you are feeling you have got a compensation ceiling in your current work, it may be time to explore for higher-paying work openings.

CHAPTER SEVEN

Investing Basics

Understanding the Fundamentals of Investing

By grasping the fundamentals of investing, setting clear goals, understanding risk, diversifying your portfolio, and staying informed, you can embark on a successful investment journey that aligns with your financial objectives and risk profile. Note that investing involves a degree of uncertainty and risk, so always seek advice from financial professionals and conduct thorough research before making investment decisions.

1. Setting Clear Investment Goals:
Before diving into investing, it's crucial to define your investment goals. Whether it is long-term wealth accumulation, retirement planning, buying a home, or funding your child's education plan, having clear motives will guide your investment decisions.

2. Risk Tolerance and Asset Allocation:
Understanding your risk tolerance is very important. Are you comfy with market fluctuations, or do you prefer more stable investments? Asset allocation involves diversifying your portfolio across various

asset classes, such as stocks, bonds, real estate, and cash, to manage risk effectively.

3. Knowledge of Different Investment Vehicles:
Learn about different investment options, including stocks, bonds, mutual funds, exchange-traded funds (ETFs), real estate, and alternative investment such as commodities and cryptocurrencies or blockchain. Each asset class has its risk-return profile, liquidity, and tax implications.

4. Investment Strategy:
Build an investment strategy that match up with your goals, risk tolerance, and time horizon. Consider if you want to be an active investor, selecting individual stocks and securities, or a passive investor, opting for index funds or ETFs to track the market.

5. Understanding Market Fundamentals:
Familiarize yourself with fundamental concepts like market cycles, economic indicators, company financials, valuation metrics, and risk factors. This knowledge will help you make informed investment decisions based on thorough analysis and research.

6. Diversification:
The adage "Don't put all your eggs in one basket" holds true in investing. Diversification spreads risk across different investments to reduce the impact of

volatility on your portfolio. Embrace risk management in all your investment. It can help protect your investments during market downturns.

7. Monitoring and Rebalancing:
Regularly monitor your investments to assess performance, review your asset allocation, and rebalance your portfolio if necessary. Rebalancing involves adjusting your holdings to maintain the desired risk-return profile based on changing market conditions.

8. Costs and Fees:
Be mindful of investment costs and fees, including expense ratios, trading commissions, management fees, and taxes. Minimizing costs can significantly affect your investment returns over time, so opt for low-cost investment options when possible.

9. Long-Term Perspective:
Investing is a long-term endeavor. While short-term market fluctuations are inevitable, staying focused on your long-term goals and avoiding knee-jerk reactions to market volatility is important for wealth accumulation and financial stability.

10. Continuous Learning:
The investment landscape is dynamic and ever-evolving. Stay enlightened about market trends, economic developments, regulatory changes, and investment strategies through books, courses, seminars, and reputable financial news sources to

enhance your knowledge and decision-making skills.

Different investment options: stocks, bonds, mutual funds, real estate

Investing is an important aspect of financial planning, allowing individuals to build their wealth over time. There are different investment options available, each with its own characteristics, risk levels, and potential returns. Here's an extensive overview of some common investment options:

Stocks
Stocks represent ownership in a company. When you buy stocks, you become a shareholder, entitling you to a portion of the company's profits (dividends) and potential capital gains if the stock price increases.
Stocks are known for their potential for high returns, but they also come with higher volatility and risk. Prices can fluctuate significantly in response to market conditions, company performance, economic factors, and investor sentiment.
Investors can choose from a wide range of stocks, including individual company stocks, exchange-traded funds (ETFs), and index funds.

Bonds
Bonds are debt securities issued by governments, municipalities, or corporations to raise capital.
When one buy a bond, you are essentially lending

money to the issuer in exchange for periodic interest payments and the return of the principal amount at maturity.

Bonds are generally considered safer than stocks because they offer a fixed income stream and have a predetermined maturity date. However, they also carry risks such as interest rate risk, credit risk, and inflation risk.

Types of bonds include government bonds, corporate bonds, municipal bonds, and treasury bonds.

Mutual Funds

Mutual funds pool money from multiple investors to invest in a diversified portfolio of stocks, bonds, or other assets. They are managed by professional portfolio managers, who make investment decisions on behalf of the investors.

Mutual funds offer diversification, as they invest in a variety of securities, reducing the impact of individual stock or bond performance on the overall portfolio.

There are different types of mutual funds, including equity funds, bond funds, index funds, balanced funds, and sector funds, catering to various investment objectives and risk preferences.

Real Estate

Real estate investment involves purchasing properties (such as residential, commercial, or industrial properties) with the aim of generating rental income and/or capital appreciation.

Real estate investments can provide steady cash flow through rental income, as well as potential long-term appreciation in property values. They also offer diversification benefits, as they have a low correlation with other asset classes like stocks and bonds.

However, real estate investments require substantial capital, ongoing maintenance costs, and may be illiquid compared to other investment options.

Commodities
Commodities are physical goods such as gold, silver, oil, agricultural products, and precious metals. Investors can gain exposure to commodities through various means, including futures contracts, commodity ETFs, and commodity mutual funds.

Commodities offer diversification benefits and can serve as a hedge against inflation and currency fluctuations. However, they can be volatile and subject to supply and demand dynamics, geopolitical factors, and commodity-specific risks.

Cryptocurrencies
Cryptocurrencies are digital or virtual currencies that use cryptography for security and operate on decentralized networks based on blockchain technology. Bitcoin, Ethereum, and Ripple are examples of popular cryptocurrencies.

Cryptocurrencies offer the potential for high returns, but they are also highly volatile and speculative.

They are not regulated by any central authority, which increases their risk profile.
Investors should exercise caution and conduct thorough research before investing in cryptocurrencies, as their prices can be influenced by factors such as market sentiment, regulatory developments, and technological advancements.

Alternative Investments
Alternative investments encompass a wide range of assets beyond traditional stocks, bonds, and real estate. These may include hedge funds, private equity, venture capital, commodities, collectibles, and derivatives.
Alternative investments often have low correlation with traditional asset classes, providing diversification benefits and potentially enhancing risk-adjusted returns. However, they can be complex, illiquid, and require a higher level of expertise to evaluate and manage effectively.
Due diligence is important when considering alternative investments, as they may involve higher fees, limited transparency, and unique risks that may not be present in traditional investments.

When choosing investment options, it's essential to consider factors such as investment goals, risk tolerance, time horizon, and diversification needs. A well-diversified portfolio typically includes a mix of different asset classes to manage risk and maximize returns over the long term. Additionally, seeking professional financial advice can help investors navigate the complexities of the investment landscape and make informed decisions aligned with their financial objectives.

Assessing risk tolerance and setting investment goals

Here are the guide to setting financial goals and assessing risk tolerance:

Step 1: Decide Your Vision for the Future
The first step to characterizing your money-related objectives is to decide your monetary vision:
what do you need your life to see like financially?
You might as of now have a clear vision in your head, but in the event that you're battling, it makes a difference to do a few contemplations.
What do you need your life to see like within the next few years?
Do you need to have a home?
Do you need to resign early?
Do you need to send your children through college?
Do you want to lower your expenses?
Make beyond any doubt to form these objectives particular and measurable. This implies characterizing your time skyline, as well as how much cash you will require, for your objectives.
For instance, on the off chance that you need to spare on expenses following year, this would result in a distinctive arrangement than somebody needing to spare for retirement in 10+ years.

Step 2: Characterize Your Time Skyline for Your Goal

When you set objectives, it's important to characterize your time skyline for the goals. The time horizon refers to the length of time you have got in order to attain your goals. How long are you progressing to grant yourself to achieve what you are attempting to get done? On the off chance that you have got a long time skyline, at that point you will be able a longer, more systematic approach. On the off chance that you have got a brief time horizon, at that point you will be constrained to require a more exceptional or prompt approach

Step 3: Decide How Much Cash You Would like Your Goals

When you are considering chance resistance and budgetary objectives you wish to figure out how much money you would like in order to realize them. On the short time that you are sparing for retirement, for illustration, you would like to know how much cash you will need to live comfortably in retirement. On the short time that an individual needs to resign in five years and they need to resign with $1million, after deciding the variables underneath, they may discover they ought to save $20,000 per year and invest that cash so that it develops over time.

Step 4: Evaluate Your Current Money related Net Worth

When investigating your hazard resilience and monetary objectives, it's vital to survey your current monetary net worth. This implies that you ought to take a stock of all of your money related accounts, counting checking, savings, speculations, credit cards, and any other advances and debts that you just have. In the event that you are not sure how to perform an essential evaluation of your money related circumstance, you will utilize an apparatus just like the Arranging instrument, which we offer complementary to our clients, to assist you survey your money related wellbeing. In the event that you're not in a position monetarily where you can really contribute within the stock showcase, at that point you will need to begin with building a crisis finance or looking for ways to extend your salary or decrease your debt.

Step 5: Survey Your Current Spending

When investigating hazard resilience and budgetary objectives it's crucial to survey your cash stream. In the event that you need to construct your riches you would like to see your current investing. A part of the individuals that I talk to admit they don't know precisely how much and where their cash is going. It's imperative to track your investing in order to plan and spare for your future objectives. This is the way you will precisely foresee your future investing and alter in like manner to meet your goals.

Step 6: Decide Your Chance Tolerance Level
The first step in deciding your chance resilience is to decide whether you're a confident person or a worry wart. If you're an optimist, at that point you accept that opportunities will show themselves which long term will be better than the show. On the off chance that that's the case, you're likely to be willing to require more hazard. On the off chance that you're a doubter, on the other hand, you accept that the long haul won't be as great as the show and are likely to want to require less risk. perfect way">The most perfect way to decide your risk resilience is to think approximately how you're feeling about money.

Your age is another factor likely to influence your risk resilience. More youthful speculators are likely to have the next chance resistance than more seasoned, more steady financial specialists. That's since youthful speculators have more time to recoup from speculation and advertise redresses. This is the time to take enormous risks since you have a bounty of time to recoup, so there's no rush.

Recap: The speculation technique you select ought to be based on your money related objectives, hazard resilience, and speculation time horizon.

Researching and selecting investments wisely

Researching and selecting investments wisely is an important aspect of achieving financial success and building wealth over time. Whether you are an experienced investor or just starting out, employing a strategic approach to investment research and selection can significantly ameliorate your chances of reaching your financial goals. Here's an extensive guide on how to research and select investments wisely:

Define Your Investment Goals
1. Start by clearly defining your investment objectives. Are you investing for retirement, purchasing a home, funding education, or seeking to make additional income?
2. Understanding your goals will help ascertain your investment horizon, risk tolerance, and the types of investments that align with your aims.

Assess Your Risk Tolerance
1. Evaluate how much risk you are willing to take with your investments. Consider factors such as your age, financial situation, investment experience, and emotional temperament.
2. Risk tolerance varies from person to person, and it's very crucial to find a balance

between risk and potential returns that you are comfortable with.

Diversification

1. Diversification is key to managing risk in your investment portfolio. Spread your investments across different asset classes, industries, and geographic regions to reduce the impact of market volatility on your overall portfolio.
2. Diversifying can help smooth out investment returns over time and mitigate the impact of poor performance in any single investment.

Conduct Thorough Research

1. Before making any investment decisions, thoroughly research the investment opportunities available to you. This includes understanding the fundamentals of the asset, its historical performance, and the market factors that may impact its future prospects.
2. Utilize a variety of sources for research, including financial news, company reports, analyst recommendations, and independent research platforms.

Understand Different Investment Vehicles

1. Familiarize yourself with the various investment options available, such as stocks, bonds, mutual funds, exchange-

traded funds (ETFs), real estate, and alternative investments.
2. Each investment vehicle has its own risk-return profile, liquidity, and tax implications, so it's essential to understand how each fits into your overall investment strategy.

Evaluate Fundamentals

1. When researching individual stocks or bonds, pay close attention to their fundamentals, including earnings growth, revenue trends, profit margins, debt levels, and management quality.
2. For real estate investments, consider factors such as location, property type, rental income potential, and market trends.

Assess Fees and Costs

1. Be careful of the fees and costs associated with different investment products. High fees can eat into your returns over time, so opt for low-cost investment options whenever possible.
2. Compare expense ratios, management fees, trading costs, and any other fees associated with the investment before making a decision.

Consider Tax Implications

1. Understand the tax implications of your investment decisions. Different investment vehicles are taxed differently, so consider

the impact of taxes on your investment returns.
2. Explore tax-efficient investment strategies, such as investing in tax-advantaged accounts like IRAs and 401(k)s, or utilizing tax-loss harvesting techniques to minimize taxes.

Stay Informed and Adapt
1. Keep yourself informed about market developments, economic trends, and regulatory changes that may affect your investments.
2. Regularly review and reassess your investment portfolio to ensure it remains aligned with your goals, risk tolerance, and market conditions.

Seek Professional Advice When Needed
1. If you are doubting about how to proceed or lack the time and experience to conduct thorough research, consider seeking advice from a qualified financial advisor.
2. A financial advisor can give personalized guidance based on your individual circumstances and help you make informed investment decisions.

By following the aforementioned guidelines and adopting a disciplined approach to researching and selecting investments wisely, you can increase the likelihood of achieving your financial objectives and building long-term wealth.

Tips for diversifying investment portfolios and monitoring performance

Diversifying your investment portfolio is very important for managing risk and maximizing returns over the long term. The following are some tips for diversifying your investment portfolio and effectively monitoring its performance:

1. Understand your risk tolerance
Before diversifying your portfolio, assess the risk tolerance. Are you comfy with aggressive growth strategies, or do you prefer a more conservative approach?
Your risk tolerance will guide your asset allocation decisions.

2. Asset allocation
Allocate your investments across various asset classes such as stocks, bonds, real estate, and commodities. Each asset class has its own risk-return profile, so spreading your investments across multiple classes can help mitigate risk.

3. Diversify within asset classes
Within each asset class, diversify further to reduce risk. For example, if you are investing in stocks,

consider diversifying across sectors (e.g., technology, healthcare, consumer goods) and company sizes (large-cap, mid-cap, small-cap).

4. Consider geographical diversification
Invest in assets from different regions and countries to reduce geographic risk. Economic and geopolitical factors can impact different regions differently, so spreading your investments globally can provide stability.

5. Use different investment strategies
Employ a mix of investment strategies such as growth investing, value investing, income investing, and market-neutral strategies. Each strategy performs differently under various market conditions, providing diversification benefits.

6. Regularly rebalance your portfolio
Rebalancing involves adjusting your portfolio's asset allocation to maintain your desired risk-return profile. Periodically review your portfolio and rebalance it by selling over performing assets and buying underperforming ones to bring your allocation back in line with your targets.

7. Monitor performance
Keep a close eye on your portfolio's performance regularly. Track key metrics such as total return, volatility, Sharpe ratio, and maximum drawdown.

Monitoring performance gives you to assess whether your investments are meeting your financial objectives and adjust your strategy if necessary.

8. Stay informed
Stay informed about market trends, economic indicators, and geopolitical developments that could impact your investments. Regularly read financial news, research reports, and market analyses to make informed decisions about your portfolio.

9. Utilize technology and tools
Take advantage of investment tracking tools, portfolio management software, and financial apps to monitor your portfolio more efficiently. These tools can provide real-time updates, performance analytics, and personalized insights to aid you make better investment decisions.

10. Seek professional counseling
Consider working with a financial advisor or investment professional to develop and manage your diversified portfolio. An experienced advisor can give personalized recommendations based on your financial goals, risk tolerance, and investment preferences.

CHAPTER EIGHT

Retirement Planning

Retirement planning is the process of setting financial goals and creating a strategy to achieve those goals in preparation for retirement. It involves determining how much money you will need to live comfortably during retirement and then saving and investing accordingly to reach that target. Retirement planning is essential for ensuring financial security and peace of mind during your retirement years.

Key components of retirement planning include:

1. Setting retirement goals
Ascertain your desired lifestyle during retirement and estimate the expenses attached to it. Consider factors such as housing, healthcare, travel, leisure activities, and any other bills you expect to incur.

2. Assessing current financial situation
Evaluate your current financial position, including your income, assets, debts, and expenses. Understanding your current financial situation will aid you determine how much you will need to save for retirement.

Kk k3. Estimating retirement savings needed

Calculate the amount of money you will need to gather by the time you retire to support your desired lifestyle. Factors to consider include inflation, life expectancy, healthcare costs, and any other financial obligations.

4. Making a retirement savings plan
Create a savings plan to reach your retirement goals. This may involve contributing to retirement accounts such as 401(k)s, IRAs, or pension plans, as well as investing in other vehicles such as stocks, bonds, mutual funds, or real estate.

5. Investment strategy
Create an investment strategy that conforms with your risk tolerance, time horizon, and financial goals. Consider diversifying your investments across different asset classes to mitigate risk and optimize returns over the long term.

6. Managing and monitoring progress
Regularly review and adjust your retirement plan as needed based on changes in your financial situation, goals, or market conditions. Monitor the investment performance and make necessary adjustments to stay on track towards your retirement goals.

7. Maximizing retirement account contributions
Take advantage of tax-advantaged retirement accounts and employer-sponsored retirement plans to maximize your contributions and tax benefits.

Consider contributing at least enough to receive any employer matching contributions.

8. Considering healthcare and long-term care needs
Factor in healthcare expenses and potential long-term care needs when planning for retirement. Explore options such as Medicare, supplemental insurance, and long-term care insurance to ensure adequate coverage.

9. Creating an estate plan
Develop an estate plan to outline how your assets will be distributed upon your death. This may involve making a will, building trusts, designating beneficiaries, and creating provisions for any dependents or heirs.

10. Seeking professional counseling
Consider working with a financial advisor or retirement planner to build and implement a comprehensive retirement plan tailored to your individual needs and circumstances. A professional can provide personalized advice and recommendations to aid you achieve your retirement objectives effectively.

The importance of retirement planning

Retirement planning is very important for achieving financial security, maintaining independence, and enjoying a comfortable lifestyle during your retirement years. It empowers you to take absolute control of your financial future, adapt to changing circumstances, and achieve your long-term goals. Retirement planning is crucial for several reasons:

1. Financial Security
Retirement planning ensures that you have enough money to maintain your desired lifestyle during retirement. It helps you accumulate sufficient savings to cover living expenses, healthcare costs, and other needs without relying solely on Social Security benefits or family support.

2. Longevity Risk
With increasing life expectancy, retirement may last for several years. Adequate retirement planning helps mitigate the risk of outliving your savings by ensuring you have enough finance to support yourself all through the retirement years.

3. Inflation Protection
Inflation takes away the purchasing power of money over a period of time. With planning and saving for retirement, you can account for inflation and ensure that your savings grow sufficiently to keep pace with rising costs of living.

4. Healthcare Costs

Healthcare expenditures tend to increase with age, and retirees often face significant medical bills. Retirement planning makes you to prepare for these expenses by setting aside funds or obtaining appropriate insurance coverage, such as Medicare or supplemental insurance.

5. Maintaining Independence

Having adequate savings through retirement planning make you to maintain independence and control over your lifestyle choices. You won't have to rely on others for financial support or sacrifice your preferences due to financial constraints.

6. Peace of Mind

Knowing that you have a solid retirement plan in place provides peace of mind and reduces financial stress. It makes you to enjoy your retirement years without worrying about running out of money or facing unforeseen financial challenges.

7. Tax Efficiency

Retirement planning entails optimizing tax strategies to reduce tax liabilities both during your working years and in retirement. Utilizing tax-advantaged retirement accounts and strategically withdrawing funds can help increase your after-tax income during retirement.

8. Legacy Planning

Retirement planning goes beyond your own financial demands and includes considerations for leaving a legacy for your loved ones or charitable causes. Proper estate planning ensures that your assets are distributed according to your wishes and minimizes tax implications for your heirs.

9. Adapting to Changing Circumstances
Life is unpredictable, and circumstances may change unexpectedly. Retirement planning entails regularly reviewing and adjusting your plan to account for changes in goals, financial situation, market conditions, and life events such as marriage, divorce, or the birth of children.

10. Social Security Optimization
Retirement planning includes strategies to optimize Social Security benefits by timing your claim to maximize lifetime benefits. Understanding Social Security rules and incorporating them into your retirement plan can significantly improve your financial security in retirement.

Assessing retirement needs and lifestyle expectations

Assessing retirement needs and lifestyle expectations is an essential aspect of retirement planning that requires careful consideration and thorough analysis. As individuals approach retirement age, it becomes imperative to evaluate various factors to ensure financial security and a comfortable lifestyle during their golden years.

1. Financial Evaluation

The first step in assessing retirement needs is to conduct a comprehensive financial evaluation. It involves calculating current assets, savings, investments, and anticipated income streams such as pensions, Social Security benefits, and any other retirement accounts. Understanding one's financial standing provides a baseline for determining retirement goals and the feasibility of achieving them.

2. Expenses Analysis

Estimating future expenses is very important in planning retirement finances. Individuals should consider both essential expenses (such as housing, healthcare, food, and utilities) and discretionary expenses (travel, leisure activities, hobbies). It is essential to account for potential inflation and healthcare costs, which tend to rise with age. Tracking current expenditures can provide insights into future spending patterns.

3. Lifestyle Expectations

Retirement is not only about financial security; it's also about fulfilling lifestyle expectations. People have various visions of retirement, ranging from travel and leisure to volunteer work and pursuing hobbies. Assessing lifestyle expectations involves envisioning how one wants to spend their time during retirement and estimating associated costs.

4. Healthcare Needs

Healthcare expenses often go up with age, making it important to factor in potential medical costs during retirement. It includes expenditures for insurance premiums, copayments, deductibles, prescription drugs, and long-term care. Assessing healthcare demands and budgeting accordingly can help avoid financial strain later on.

5. Longevity Considerations

With rising life expectancy, retirement planning needs to account for the possibility of a longer retirement period. Individuals should consider how many years they expect to spend in retirement and ensure their financial resources can sustain them for the whole of this time. Planning for longevity may involve adjusting investment strategies and savings targets.

6. Debt Management

Paying off debt before retirement can significantly ameliorate financial stability during retirement. High-interest debt, such as credit card debt or loans, can erode savings and limit financial flexibility. Assessing debt levels and creating a plan to pay off outstanding balances can eradicate financial stress in retirement.

7. Social Security and Pension Benefits

Understanding the benefits available through Social Security and any employer-sponsored pension plans is essential for retirement planning. Individuals should assess their eligibility, estimated benefits, and the optimal timing for claiming these benefits. Maximizing Social Security benefits and pension payouts can enhance retirement income.

8. Risk Tolerance and Investment Strategy
Assessing risk tolerance is essential for checking an appropriate investment strategy for retirement savings. Younger individuals may have a higher risk tolerance and can afford to allocate a larger portion of their portfolio to growth-oriented investments. As retirement approaches, individuals may go for more conservative investment strategies to protect accumulated wealth.

9. Contingency Planning
Unexpected events such as market downturns, health emergencies, or changes in family circumstances can impact retirement plans. Building an emergency fund and having appropriate insurance coverage (such as health insurance, long-term care insurance, and life insurance) can provide a safety net during challenging times.

10. Regular Review and Adjustment
Retirement planning is not a one-time activity; it requires ongoing review and adjustment. As circumstances change, such as shifts in income, expenses, or investment performance, individuals

should revisit their retirement plan regularly and make necessary modifications to ensure it remains aligned with their goals and expectations.

Retirement account options: 401(k), Roth IRA, etc.

When planning for retirement, individuals have access to a variety of retirement account options that offer tax advantages, investment opportunities, and flexibility. Each retirement account option has its own features, contribution limits, tax implications, and eligibility requirements. It's important to check your financial goals, income level, and employment situation to ascertain which retirement accounts suit your retirement savings strategy. Consulting with a financial advisor can also aid you navigate the complexities of retirement planning and optimize your savings across various account types for a secure retirement future.
The following are some common retirement account options to consider:

401(k)
1. Traditional 401(k)
A traditional 401(k) is an employer-sponsored retirement plan that gives room for employees to contribute pre-tax dollars to their retirement account. Contributions grow tax-deferred until withdrawal in retirement, at which point they are taxed as ordinary income.

2. Roth 401(k)

A Roth 401(k) enjoin features of a traditional 401(k) with a Roth IRA. Contributions are made with after-tax dollars, but withdrawals in retirement, including earnings, are tax-free if certain conditions are met. Employers may offer a match on Roth 401(k) contributions similar to a traditional 401(k).

Individual Retirement Account (IRA)

1. Traditional IRA

A traditional IRA gives room for individuals to contribute pre-tax dollars to his or her retirement account, potentially lowering their taxable income. Earnings grow tax-deferred until withdrawal in retirement, where they are taxed as ordinary income.

2. Roth IRA

A Roth IRA requires after-tax contributions, but qualified withdrawals in retirement, including earnings, are tax-free. Roth IRAs offer more flexibility in terms of investment choices and withdrawal options.

SEP IRA (Simplified Employee Pension IRA)

A SEP IRA is a retirement plan designed for self-employed individuals or small business owners. Contributions are tax-deductible and grow tax-deferred until withdrawal. SEP IRAs have higher contribution limits than traditional IRAs, making them attractive for those with variable income.

Simple IRA (Savings Incentive Match Plan for Employees)
A Simple IRA is designed for small businesses with fewer than 100 employees. Both employers and employees can make contributions to the account. Contributions are tax-deductible, and earnings grow tax-deferred until withdrawal.

Solo 401(k) or Individual 401(k)
Designed for self-employed individuals with no employees (other than a spouse), a Solo 401(k) allows for both employee and employer contributions. Solo 401(k) plans offer higher contribution limits and more investment options compared to other retirement accounts.

457 Plan
A 457 plan is a retirement savings account available to state and local government employees and some nonprofit organizations. Contributions are typically pre-tax, and withdrawals in retirement are taxed as ordinary income.

403(b) Plan
A 403(b) plan is a retirement account available to employees of certain nonprofit organizations, public schools, and other tax-exempt organizations. Contributions are often tax-deferred, and investment options may include annuities and mutual funds.

Health Savings Account (HSA)

While primarily used for healthcare expenses, an HSA can also serve as a retirement savings vehicle. Contributions are tax-deductible, grow tax-free, and withdrawals for qualified medical expenses are tax-free. After age 65, non-medical withdrawals are taxed as ordinary income.

Strategies for Maximizing Retirement Contributions and Employer Matches

1. Understand Your Retirement Plan
Initiate by familiarizing yourself with your employer-sponsored retirement plan, such as a 401(k) or 403(b). Understand the contribution limits, investment options, employer match policy, and vesting schedule to maximize your retirement savings potential.

2. Contribute at Least Enough to Get the Full Match
Take advantage of your employer's matching contributions. Contribute at least enough to meet the match threshold, as this is importantly free money that robust your retirement savings without any additional input on your part.

3. Increase Your Contributions Over Time
Gradually upgrade your contributions to your retirement account as your income grows or when you receive a bonus or raise. Aim to maximize your

annual contribution limit to take full advantage of tax-deferred growth and compound interest.

4. Take Advantage of Catch-Up Contributions

If you are 50 years or above, consider making catch-up contributions to your retirement account. These additional contributions make older individuals save more for retirement and benefit from higher contribution limits than younger savers.

5. Opt for Automatic Payroll Deductions

Set up automatic payroll deductions to contribute a portion of your salary directly to your retirement account before you have a chance to spend it. This method ensures consistent savings and helps you avoid the temptation to spend the money elsewhere.

6. Reassess Your Budget and Prioritize Savings

Reassess your budget to identify areas where you can cut back on expenses and redirect those funds towards retirement savings. Prioritize saving for retirement as a non-negotiable expense to secure your financial future.

7. Diversify Your Investments

Allocate your retirement contributions across a diverse mix of investment options based on your risk tolerance, time horizon, and financial goals. Diversification can help mitigate risk and optimize returns over the long term.

8. Monitor and Rebalance Your Portfolio
Regularly review your retirement account's performance and asset allocation. Rebalance your portfolio periodically to realign with your investment objectives, risk tolerance, and market conditions to maximize growth potential and minimize risk.

9. Consider Roth IRA Contributions
In addition to your employer-sponsored retirement plan, consider contributing to a Roth IRA. While contributions to a Roth IRA are not tax-deductible, withdrawals in retirement are tax-free, providing tax diversification and flexibility in retirement income planning.

10. Consult with a Financial Advisor
Seek guidance from a financial advisor to create a comprehensive retirement savings strategy tailored to your individual circumstances. An advisor can help you optimize contributions, investment options, tax strategies, and retirement income planning to maximize your savings potential.

By leveraging these strategies for maximizing retirement contributions and taking advantage of employer matches, you can enhance your retirement savings, build a robust nest egg, and secure a financially stable future. Consistent savings discipline, prudent investment decisions, and proactive retirement planning are key to achieving long-term financial security and a comfortable retirement lifestyle.

Tips for Managing and Optimizing Retirement Investments

Managing and optimizing your retirement investments is essential to make sure financial security during your retirement years. The following are some of the tips that will of help in maximizing the growth and sustainability of your retirement portfolio:

1. Set Clear Goals and Develop a Plan
Defining your retirement goals, including your dream lifestyle, retirement age, and income needs. Developing a comprehensive retirement plan that considers your timeline, risk tolerance, and investment strategies to achieve the financial objectives.

2. Diversify Your Investment Portfolio
Spread your investments across different asset classes (stocks, bonds, real estate) to minimize risk and increase opportunities for growth.
Consider diversification within each asset class to further control risk.

3. Regularly Review and Rebalance Your Portfolio
Review your investments periodically to ensure they conform with your goals and risk tolerance.
Reevaluate your portfolio as demanded to maintain your desired asset allocation and risk level.

4. Consider Tax-Efficient Strategies

Maximize contributions to tax-advantaged retirement accounts such as 401(k), IRA, or Roth IRA to benefit from tax-deferred or tax-free growth.
Use tax-loss harvesting and tax-efficient investments to minimize tax liabilities on your investment gains.

5. Control Investment Costs

Choose low-cost investment options, such as index funds or ETFs, to minimize expenditure and increase your overall returns.
Avoid frequent trading and excessive fees that can erode your investment returns over time.

6. Stay Informed and Educated

Keep yourself informed about market trends, economic indicators, and financial news that may affect your investments.
Educate yourself on investment strategies, retirement planning, and ways to optimize your portfolio to make informed decisions.

7. Consider Professional guidance

Consult with a financial advisor or planner to receive personalized counseling on retirement planning, investment strategies, and risk management.
Seek advice from experienced personnel who can help you navigate complex financial decisions and optimize your retirement investments.

8. Plan for Long-Term Growth and Income
Invest with a long-term perspective to benefit from compounding growth and withstand fluctuations in market.
Build a diversified portfolio that balances growth investments with income-producing assets to support your retirement lifestyle.

9. Tailor Your Plan as Demanded
Regularly review your retirement plan and adjust your investments based on changing life circumstances, market conditions, and financial goals.

CHAPTER NINE

Protecting Your Financial Future

Protecting your financial future is essential to safeguard your assets, income, and overall financial well-being against unforeseen events and risks. By actively safeguarding and monitoring your financial situation, you can protect your financial future, create wealth, and achieve long-term financial security and stability for yourself and your loved ones.

Importance of insurance coverage for various aspects of life

Insurance coverage plays an essential role in different aspects of life by enabling financial protection and peace of mind. However, insurance coverage helps individuals and families mitigate financial risks, maintain financial stability, and protect their assets and well-being in various aspects of life.

These are the reason why insurance is important in different areas of life:

Health Insurance
Covers medical expenses, enabling access to quality healthcare without significant financial stress in case of illness or medical mishap.

Life Insurance
Provision of financial support to beneficiaries in the event of the policyholder's death, aiding to cover funeral expenses, replace lost income, pay off debts, keep and protect the family's standard of living.

Auto Insurance
Protects against financial mishap due to accidents, theft, or damage to vehicles, as well as liability for injuries or damages caused to others in accidents.

Homeowners/Renters Insurance
Protects against financial losses from damages to property due to disasters, theft, or liability claims, ensuring repair or replacement costs are taken care of.

Disability Insurance
Provides income replacement if the policyholder becomes unable to work due to a disability or dependability, ensuring ongoing financial stability.

Business Insurance
Safeguard businesses from financial losses due to property damage, liability claims, or interruption of operations, helping to protect investments and ensure continuity.

Travel Insurance

Enables coverage for unexpected events during travel, such as trip cancellations, medical emergencies, or lost luggage, reducing financial risks while away from home.

Veterinary Insurance
Covers domestic animals or pet expenses, ensuring they receive necessary medical care without the burden of high costs.

Assessing risk tolerance and choosing appropriate coverage

Assessing risk tolerance is important when selecting insurance coverage to ensure it conforms with your financial situation, goals, and comfort level with risk. By meticulously evaluating risk tolerance and choosing appropriate coverage, you can effectively manage financial risks while protecting your assets, income, and well-being against unforeseen circumstances.
These are guides to help choose appropriate coverage based on risk tolerance:

Evaluate Financial Situation
Understand your current financial standing, including income, assets, debts, and expenses. Consider how much you can comfortably allocate towards insurance premiums without straining your budget.

Assess Risk Tolerance

Determine your readiness to take on risk. Are you more conservative, preferring greater protection even if it means higher premiums?
Or are you comfortable with some level of risk to potentially save on premiums?

Consider Insurance Needs
Identify areas where insurance coverage is necessary based on your lifestyle, responsibilities, and potential risks. This could include health, life, auto, home, disability, and liability insurance.

Understand Coverage Options
Research different types of insurance policies available and their coverage limits, deductibles, and exclusions. Compare the returns and costs of each option to find the right balance between coverage and affordability.

Evaluate Risk Factors
Evaluate specific risk factors that may affect your insurance needs, such as age, health status, occupation, location, and lifestyle habits. Adjust coverage levels accordingly to address potential risks.

Review Policy Terms
Meticulously reviews policy terms and conditions, including coverage limits, deductibles, exclusions, and claim procedures. Ensure the policy provides adequate protection for potential risks while

avoiding unnecessary coverage that may not align with your needs.

Seek Professional Guidance
Consider consulting with insurance agents, financial advisors, or risk management experts for personalized advice. They can help assess your risk tolerance, recommend appropriate coverage options, and tailor insurance solutions to your specific needs and goals.

Regularly Review Coverage
Occasionally reevaluate your insurance demands and coverage levels as your financial situation and life circumstances change. Update your policies accordingly to ensure you maintain adequate safeguard against evolving risks.

Protecting assets through estate planning and will preparation

Protecting assets via estate planning and will preparation involves different strategies to ensure your assets are distributed according to your wishes while minimizing taxes and legal complications. This may include creating a will, establishing trusts, designating beneficiaries for accounts and policies, and considering asset protection techniques such as insurance and gifting. Consulting with legal and financial experts who can help tailor a plan that matches your specific demands and goals.

CHAPTER TEN

Building Generational Wealth

This refers to the strategic accumulation of assets, resources, and financial security over time with the intention of providing long-term benefits for future generations within a family or community. It involves making informed financial decisions, investing wisely, and implementing effective estate planning strategies to ensure that wealth is preserved and passed down to heirs or beneficiaries across multiple generations. Building generational wealth often involves a combination of prudent financial management, asset allocation, education, and legacy planning to create a lasting financial legacy that can support future generations' economic stability, opportunities, and quality of life.

Strategies for passing on wealth to future generations

Passing on wealth to future generations requires meticulous planning and consideration. These strategies need to be considered:

Estate Planning
Build a comprehensive estate plan that includes a will, trusts, and other legal instruments to specify how your assets will be distributed after your

passing. This can help minimize estate taxes and ensure your wishes are carried out.

Trusts
Establish trusts to hold and manage assets for the benefit of your heirs or wealth beneficiaries. Trusts can provide flexibility in distributing assets over time, guard assets from creditors and lawsuits, and minimize estate taxes.

Gifting
Make use of the annual gift tax exclusion to gift assets to your heirs tax-free up to a certain amount each year. This can help minimize the size of your estate while providing financial support to your loved ones during your lifetime.

Education Funding
Create education savings accounts, such as 529 plans, to help fund the educational expenses of your children or grandchildren. These accounts offer tax advantages and can help ensure that future generations have access to quality education.

Family Limited Partnerships
Consider building a family limited partnership to hold and manage family assets. This can provide asset protection, centralized management, and facilitate the transfer of ownership interests to future generations.

Life Insurance

Buy life insurance policies to provide liquidity for estate taxes or to equalize inheritances among heirs. Life insurance returns can also gives financial support to your heirs and beneficiaries.

Charitable Giving

Incorporate charitable giving into your estate plan by establishing charitable trusts or making bequests to charitable organizations. This can help minimize estate taxes and leave a legacy of philanthropy for future generations.

Financial Education

Enlighten your heirs about financial literacy, investment principles, and wealth management strategies. By empowering and equipping them with the knowledge and skills to manage and control their inheritance responsibly, you can help ensure the long-term preservation of family wealth.

Open Dialogue

Foster open communication within your family about wealth, inheritance, and financial values. Discussing extensively your opinions and expectations can help prevent misunderstandings and conflicts among heirs.

Teaching financial literacy and values to children

Teaching financial literacy and values to children is essential for their future success. Start with basic concepts like saving, budgeting, and the importance of delayed gratification. Use real-life examples and involve them in family financial discussions. Encourage them to set savings goals and earn money through chores or part-time jobs. Moreso, instill values like responsible spending, giving back to the community, and understanding the difference between needs and wants. Consistency and leading by example are key in this process.

Philanthropy and giving back to the community

Philanthropy and giving back to the community Teaching children about philanthropy and giving back to the community helps foster empathy, compassion, and a sense of social responsibility. Encourage them to volunteer their time, donate toys or clothes they no longer need, or participate in fundraising activities for charitable causes.

Discuss the impact of their actions on others and emphasize the importance of helping those in need. Lead by example by engaging in philanthropic activities as a family and highlighting the joy and fulfillment that comes from giving back.

Creating a lasting legacy and impact through financial success

Creating a lasting legacy and impact through financial success involves not only accumulating wealth but also utilizing it to positively influence others and society. This can include philanthropy, investing in sustainable businesses, supporting education and healthcare initiatives, and leaving a meaningful inheritance for future generations. It's about leveraging your resources to make a lasting difference in the world and leaving a positive mark long after you're gone.

Understanding the Significance:

Creating a lasting legacy through financial success goes beyond personal gain. It involves leveraging resources and wealth to make a positive impact that endures beyond one's lifetime.

By conscientiously managing finances and investments, individuals can build foundations, fund charitable initiatives, support communities, and catalyze change in society.

Through strategic planning and responsible stewardship of wealth, one can leave behind a legacy that not only benefits future generations but also contributes to the greater good of humanity.

Conclusion

Embracing Financial Mastery

As we conclude our journey through "The Ultimate Blueprint of Mastering Money: Practical Strategies for Financial Success," it becomes clear that true financial mastery is not just about accumulating wealth but about using it wisely to shape a legacy that transcends generations.

Throughout this book, we have explored practical strategies for achieving financial success, emphasizing the importance of budgeting, investing wisely, and cultivating a mindset of abundance. We have delved into the power of compounding interest, the significance of diversification, and the impact of financial literacy on our long-term prosperity.

However, beyond the accumulation of wealth lies a deeper purpose – the opportunity to create a lasting impact through our financial success. By aligning our financial goals with our values, we can shape a legacy that reflects our deepest convictions and aspirations.

As we implement the lessons learned from this blueprint, let us remember that true wealth is not measured by the size of our bank accounts but by the positive influence we exert on the world around us. Let us strive to be stewards of our resources, using them to uplift others, support causes we believe in, and leave a legacy that will endure far beyond our own lifetimes.

In closing, may this book serve as a compass on your journey to financial mastery, guiding you towards a future marked by prosperity, purpose, and profound impact. Embrace the power of financial success not just for personal gain, but as a pathway to creating a legacy that will stand the test of time.